# TEXAS
## CROSSWORDS

**Crosswords, Wordfinds & More**

DALE RATERMANN & LANA BANDY

Dedicated to Sanchez:
Pizza, peanut butter, and watermelon, oh my!

Texas Crosswords: Crosswords, Wordfinds & More
Copyright © 2021 by Dale Ratermann, Lana Bandy

Published by Blue River Press
Indianapolis, Indiana
www.brpressbooks.com

Distributed by Cardinal Publishers Group
A Tom Doherty Company, Inc.
www.cardinalpub.com

All rights reserved under International and Pan-American Copyright Conventions.

No part of this book may be reproduced, stored in a database or other retrieval system, or transmitted in any form, by any means, including mechanical, photocopy, recording or otherwise, without the prior written permission of the publisher.

ISBN: 978-1-68157-143-0

Cover Design: Scott Lohr
Cover Photos: CrackerClips Stock Media / Shutterstock, Sean Pavone / Shutterstock, Semisatch / Shutterstock
Editor: Dani McCormick
Interior Design: Dani McCormick

Printed in the United States of America

10 9 8 7 6 5 4 3 2 1     21 22 23 24 25 26 27 28 29 30

| | |
|---|---|
| **Introduction** | v |
| **Part I:** Texas People | |
| Famous Texans | 2 |
| Texas Entertainers | 10 |
| Musical Performers | 18 |
| Texas Women | 24 |
| Texas Politicians | 30 |
| Texas Writers | 36 |
| Texas Business | 42 |
| Sports in Texas | 49 |
| **Part II:** Texas Regions | |
| The Panhandle | 64 |
| North Central | 70 |
| East | 74 |
| South | 84 |
| Central | 92 |
| West | 100 |
| **Part III:** Texas Activities | |
| "Amused" in Texas | 109 |
| Texas Fauna | 114 |
| Texas Flora | 120 |
| Texas Festivals | 124 |
| Texas Arts | 128 |
| Texas History | 133 |
| **Answer Key** | 139 |

Don't mess with Texas,
Everything's bigger here:
T–E–X–A–S.

—Carlton T. Chapman

# Introduction

Put simply, the state of Texas is diverse. The people are as diverse as the landscape. And the rich history is as diverse as the twenty-first-century lifestyle.

From El Paso to Beaumont. From Guadalupe Peak to the Gulf of Mexico shores. And from farmlands to city skyscrapers.

This book will explore the people, places and activities that have made Texas the great state that it has been for nearly 175 years.

Each chapter is filled with stories and puzzles to test your knowledge of The Lone Star State. Hopefully, you will be entertained, amused, and educated.

There are challenges for readers of all ages, whether you are a lifelong native or a recent transplant, an urban dweller or a country charmer.

Texas is a wonderful place to explore. Hike the trails, sail the waterways, bike the country roads, and wander the cities.

Texas is the state of "Friendship." Enjoy the journey.

# Part I:
# Texas People

Texas Crosswords

# Famous Texans

From Oscar-winning actors to US presidents and business icons, Texas has been to home to some very famous people.

Four US presidents had ties to Texas, including George H.W. and George W. Bush. Dwight Eisenhower was born in the state and Lyndon Johnson was a lifelong Texan. Actors Matthew McConaughey, Owen and Luke Wilson, and Jamie Foxx all hail from Texas, as do Forest Whitaker and Tommy Lee Jones. Foxx was born in Terrell and attended Terrell High School. He played basketball and football and sang and played the piano at his church New Hope Baptist. He started playing the piano at age five. This dedication paid off in 2004 when he won the Best Actor Oscar for his work in Ray as Ray Charles.

Actresses Carol Burnett and Jennifer Garner were born in Texas, as were Academy Award winners Sissy Spacek and Renee Zellweger. Spacek was born and raised in Quitman. She attended Quitman High School, where she was named homecoming queen. Spacek won the 1980 Oscar for Best Actress for her part as Loretta Lynn in Coal Miner's Daughter. She has five other Best Actress nominations. Perhaps her best-known role was as the title character in Carrie (1976), a high school girl with telekinetic powers.

Texas is well known for its musical heritage. In the 1970s, country music invaded Austin, but it had a new sound. "Outlaw" or alternative country stars such as Willie Nelson, Steve Earle, Jerry Jeff Walker, and Waylon Jennings emerged. Other country acts from Texas include George Strait, Kenny Rogers, Kris Kristofferson, and Miranda Lambert.

Pop stars Selena Gomez, Jessica Simpson, Hillary Duff, Kelly Clarkson, and Demi Lovato are all from Texas, as are Beyonce and Ciara.

# Part I: Texas People

Stevie Ray Vaughan, Buddy Holly, and Roy Orbison are American music legends. Vaughan was an amazing blues guitarist and a member of the band Double Trouble. He had a short-lived but impressive career, winning six Grammy awards. He died at the age of 35 in a 1990 helicopter crash. There is a memorial statue of Vaughan in Austin.

Heavyweight fighter George Foreman was born in Marshall and grew up in Fifth Ward, Houston. Foreman is also known as the spokesman for the George Foreman Grill, which has earned him more money than his boxing career.

In the sports world, some of Texas's most famous stars include baseballer Nolan Ryan, cyclist Lance Armstrong, and football players Drew Brees and Adrian Peterson.

Fashion designer Tom Ford was born in Austin. Billionaires Ross Perot and Howard Hughes were born in the state, as was TV producer Aaron Spelling.

Beyoncé, born and raised in Houston, Texas, is one of the world's top-selling musical artists with over 118 million records sold worldwide.

# Texas Crosswords

# Famous Texans Crossword

Solution on page 138.

## Across

1. Attention-getter
5. I-20 exits
10. Unshakable Grounds coffee
14. Actress Moore
15. PayPal funds
16. Mideast land
17. "___ Yankees"
18. Caffe Medici order
19. Sword handle

## Down

1. Puts two and two together
2. Mavericks foe
3. Labor leader Tenayuca
4. Petty detail
5. Kick back at Horseshoe Bay Resort
6. Texas thorny plant
7. Allen HS subject
8. Two hours behind CST

# Part I: Texas People

## Across (cont.)

20. Heisman Trophy winner and Super Bowl MVP
22. Boredom
23. IAH-to-hotel connection
24. Rodeo Austin ropes
26. Comet Cleaners challenge
29. NASA program
31. SW Indian
33. Seek treatment at Kindred Hospital
34. Barely beats the Texans
38. Adaptable truck, for short
39. First woman to serve on the US Supreme Court
42. Taste a Tap Exchange ale
43. Wire fence sticker
45. Texas Poet Laureate's preposition
46. John H. Kirby State Forest lumberjack's cry
48. Functional
51. Fort Worth Garden Club bloomer
52. Like the Dash for the Beads and Puppy Love 5K
55. Gulf port
57. Absurd
58. Anchorman on CBS for 19 years
62. Icy coating
63. Angry look
65. WFAA's American ____
66. Leave in, to a Texas Monthly editor
67. LA's region
68. 58-Across delivered it
69. Texas A&M exam
70. Adhesive
71. Hamlet, e.g.

## Down (cont.)

9. Willie Nelson: "____ Is Gone"
10. 36th US President
11. Kind of acid
12. Texas hardware stores: True ____
13. Nay sayers
21. Steve Martin's instrument
22. Night school course, initially
24. Raider Red Meats cut
25. Apportion
26. Rudely ignore
27. "Bye-bye!"
28. Allege in Archer County Court
30. Discussion group
32. Indian, for one
35. University of Texas Press 13-digit ID
36. Oxbow Bakery array
37. Like a Rice cheerleader
40. McDonald Observatory spheres
41. Turn red, maybe
44. Comedienne who received a Life Achievement Award from the Screen Actors Guild in 2016
47. Human race (un-PC)
49. Take to Floyd County Court
50. Q-Tip target
52. Top spot in the Big 12 Conference
53. Bring together
54. Baylor football team roster entries
56. Two Men and a Truck cart
58. Designer Chanel
59. Texas Public Policy Foundation nugget
60. Dot on a Texas map
61. "If all ____ fails…"
63. Amarillo-to-Abilene dir.
64. Texas State Police officer

# Texas Crosswords

## Martin Sudoku

Use logic to fill in the boxes so every row, column and 2x3 box contains the letters M-A-R-T-I-N, in honor of Mary Martin. The actress/singer was a native of Weatherford and won a Tony Award, an Emmy Award, a Kennedy Center Honor and was inducted into the American Theater Hall of Fame. Solution on page 138.

|   | M |   |   |   | I |
|---|---|---|---|---|---|
|   | A |   | R |   |   |
| M |   |   | A |   | T |
| A |   | N |   |   | R |
|   | A |   | R |   |   |
| N |   |   | I |   |   |

## Wiley Post Sudoku

Use logic to fill in the grid so every row, column and 3x3 box contains the letters W–I–L–E–Y–P–O–S–T, in honor of Wiley Post. The famed aviator was born in Van Zandt County and is best known for being the first pilot to fly solo around the world. Solution on page 138.

| Y |   |   | S |   | W |   |   | O |
|---|---|---|---|---|---|---|---|---|
|   |   | I |   |   |   | E |   |   |
| O | L |   |   |   |   |   | P | S |
|   |   | O |   | P |   | Y |   |   |
|   | W |   | T |   | L |   | S |   |
|   |   | S |   | Y |   | W |   |   |
| I | P |   |   |   |   |   | L | Y |
|   |   | T |   |   |   | I |   |   |
| S |   |   | I |   | P |   |   | T |

Part I: Texas People

## Astronauts Word Search

Solution on page 138.

```
T H G U O R B M I K M B E A N
R T O K F C R E I G H T O N V
A A S C O T T I U C E R N A N
H O N M I T C H E L L E V D Q
K E S D W R E H S I F I M B E
C A E H E A N Y T Y L L R J Q
O Z Z S B R L P M U L L A N E
L L C H Q J S K F R L Y Y U G
A N A I B A F O E S I R R A H
C O C K R E L L C R I P P E N
B R M P V U Y B H S A G S U T
D L O C V E C G I V E N S Z N
U K A H O L M Q U E S T C S D
R D W H I T E N P T B E E Q M
G H K S A V I L O N T E M H E
```

| | | |
|---|---|---|
| ANDERS | FABIAN | MITCHELL |
| ASHBY | FISHER | MULLANE |
| BEAN | GIVENS | OLIVAS |
| BLAHA | HARRIS | REILLY |
| CERNAN | HOLMQUEST | SCOTT |
| COCKRELL | KIMBROUGH | SEE |
| CREIGHTON | KOPRA | WALKER |
| CRIPPEN | LOCKHART | WHITE |

# Infamous Texans Crossword

Solution on page 138.

### Across

1. Brink
5. ___ weevil
9. "Thanks," in a TCU German class
14. A single time
15. Alamo Fencing Academy weapon
16. Chirpy birds
17. Demeanor
18. Get larger
19. Sabine River wader

### Down

1. Martini Blu Jazz Cafe group
2. Confederacy foe
3. Trail for a dog
4. One of the Ivies
5. Sires, biblically
6. O of the magazine world
7. Centerville's county
8. Bawdy
9. Reside

## Part I: Texas People

### Across (cont.)

20. Outlaws portrayed by Faye along with Warren
23. Mich. neighbor
24. Degree in an SMU math class
25. The whole enchilada
26. BSA Health spots
27. Usual HS football game day
29. Really impress
33. Reach via jet
36. Miss Texas crown
38. "Yo!"
39. John F. Kennedy assassin
42. UT frat letter
43. Condemns
44. Ill will
45. 1975 Dallas WCT champ
47. Schoolboy
48. Motorists' org.
49. Sparky's Pub spigot
51. XXX/X
52. Witness
55. Ronald Reagan shooter
60. Not so hot
61. Wander
62. I-10 Rest ____
63. Jim Wells County seat
64. Austen novel
65. Little jerks
66. Sanctify
67. In public
68. Make full

### Down (cont.)

10. Common sock pattern at Austin Country Club
11. Geeky type
12. Oft-injured joint for Aggies
13. An hour earlier than CST
21. Bit of progress
22. Egyptian capital
26. Ordinal ending
27. Demonic sort
28. Rangers foes
30. Bangkok City Restaurant cuisine
31. Breton or Gael
32. Jekyll's counterpart
33. Pet peeve
34. "____ do it!"
35. Slangy assent
36. Rating for some KXAN shows
37. Attack
40. Ex-Sen. Yarborough
41. FDR program
46. Texas Tech law school course
48. Former Cowboys quarterback
50. Peruvian peaks
51. Meaning of Caesar's "veni"
52. Damascus land
53. DVD player option
54. Wipe off
55. Solidify
56. Mayberry boy
57. Angers
58. US city that is 3,788 miles from Houston
59. Dines at Turtle Restaurant
60. Cujo's Sports Bar bill

# Texas Crosswords

## Entertainers

The list of famous Texas entertainers is like a "Who's Who" of Hollywood. Several of today's top film forces got their start in the state. Numerous Academy Award winners are from Texas, including Matthew McConaughey, Jamie Foxx, Forest Whitaker, and Renee Zellweger. Sissy Spacek was a Best Actress winner, and Tommy Lee Jones was Best Supporting Actor.

Renee Zellweger was born and raised in Katy (near Houston). She was an active Katy High School student, participating in cheerleading, gymnastics, and speech. She was also a member of the drama club. While an English major at the University of Texas at Austin, Zellweger took a drama course that started her on the road to success. One of her first film roles was in 1994'S Texas Chainsaw Massacre: The Next Generation alongside fellow Texan Matthew McConaughey. Zellweger's breakout role was in Jerry Maguire, and she won her Best Supporting Actress Oscar for her part in Cold Mountain.

Tommy Lee Jones is a lifelong Texan. Born in San Saba and raised in Midland, he played football at Robert E. Lee high School and at Harvard. Jones, who won his Oscar for The Fugitive, has two Texas ranches (a 3,000-acre cattle ranch in San Saba and another in Van Horn) and a home in Terrell Hills outside San Antonio.

Movie Directors Wes Anderson, Tom Ford (yes, the fashion designer), and Richard Linklater are from Texas. Anderson was born in Houston and attended UT, where he met his friend and frequent collaborator Owen Wilson. He got his start with the film Bottle Rockets, which starred Owen and his brother Luke Wilson. Anderson's alma mater, St. John's School, played a big role in his movie Rushmore.

Beyonce is one of today's most popular singers. Born and raised in Houston, she sang in church choirs and took numerous dance classes as a youngster. She gained her fame as lead singer of the band Destiny's Child in the 1990s. She has since gone solo and earned five

Grammy awards. Beyonce's sister, Solange, is a singer as well.

Other famous entertainers from Texas include such diverse personalities as Robin Wright, Amber Heard, Dennis Quaid, Carol Burnett, Dancing with the Stars' Mark Ballas, Beavis & Butthead creator Mike Judge, Janis Joplin, Ginger Rogers, Gary Busey, Tom Jones, and Nelly.

Matthew McConaughey was born in Uvalde, Texas, but moved to Longview, Texas, at the age of eleven. He has won Academy Awards and Emmys for his outstanding on-screen performances and now lives in Austin, Texas with his wife and three children.

Texas Crosswords

# Actors Crossword
Solution on page 138.

## Across

1. Not stereo
5. Big cheese
11. KERA net.
14. Any day now
15. Texas Observer typos
16. Kenny Rogers: "All I Need is ___"
17. No. 2 vote-getter in Texas in 2000 US presidential election
18. Like Playboy cartoons

## Down

1. Chinese food additive
2. Stars shutout, in box scores
3. Edna Post Office creed word
4. Blood type, briefly
5. ___ non grata
6. Bay window
7. Eyes, poetically
8. Bexar County Fair barn cry
9. Falcons, on NRG Stadium scoreboards

12

# Part I: Texas People

## Across (cont.)

19. Briggs Ranch Golf Club ball position
20. Some are inert
22. Sensed
23. In poor health at Del Sol Medical Center
26. MSN rival
27. Exxon Mobil office note
30. Marcus' partner
32. Persevering
36. Kind of retro lamp
37. Frightened
39. Denton Community Market corn core
40. Like wine at Texas Star Winery
41. Cowboy foe
42. The Sun ___ Rises
43. Rattlesnake Ranch pecan, e.g.
44. Bone-chilling
47. Central street in many Texas towns
48. Lessens in worth
50. Not for kids
52. Changed color at Ana's Hair Salon
53. Big Apple inits.
54. Some UNT students
55. Fallon predecessor
58. Whale of a prophet
60. Larry Gatlin: "What ___ We Doin' Lonesome"
61. Give in
64. Watch face
68. TPC San Antonio org.
69. Show starring the actress found in the puzzle's circles
70. Scrabble piece
71. Boozehound
72. Silvery fish
73. Competed in the Texas Senior Games

## Down (cont.)

10. "We've been ___!"
11. Gomer of Mayberry
12. Seethe
13. It's for the birds
21. Battery size
22. I-10 driving hazard
23. Like all of West Texas
24. Astros group
25. KDFW newscast, e.g.
27. Dallas' Super Bowl VI opponent
28. A Manning
29. Center
31. "Spy vs. Spy" magazine
32. Some Texas Motorplex races
33. Showy displays
34. More intrusive
35. Govt. securities
38. Part of KFC
42. Heart Hospital doc bloc
44. Leave from Hobby Airport
45. Regret
46. Grayson Hills Winery quality
49. Brouhaha
51. Nipper's co.
53. Greet silently
55. Boyd Raceway units
56. Start of a conclusion
57. Straight, at Tradinghouse Bar
58. Come together
59. 51-Down product
61. Corsicana Daily Sun revenue source
62. Engine part
63. Indians, on Globe Life Park scoreboards
65. Sundial number
66. Liberty Tree Tavern brew
67. ___ Zeppelin

Texas Crosswords

## Murphy Sudoku

Use logic to fill in the grid so every row, column and 2x3 box contains the letters M–U–R–P–H–Y, in honor of Audie Murphy. He was born in Kingston and was one of the most decorated American combat soldiers of World War II. He became a film star and appeared in more than 40 movies. Solution on page 139.

|   |   | R |   |   |   |
|---|---|---|---|---|---|
| H | U | M |   |   |   |
|   |   | H | P | H |   |
|   | Y | M | U |   |   |
|   |   |   | P | H | U |
|   |   |   | R |   |   |

## Liza Koshy Sudoku

Use logic to fill in the boxes so every row, column and 3x3 box contains the letters L–I–Z–A–K–O–S–H–Y in honor of Liza Koshy. The YouTube personality was born and raised in Houston and stars in the Hulu television series Freakish. Solution on page 139.

| I |   |   |   | H |   | A |   |   |
|---|---|---|---|---|---|---|---|---|
|   | O |   | Y | Z |   |   | K | I |
|   |   | S | I | K |   | H |   | Z |
| Y |   |   | L |   | O | Z | I | K |
|   |   |   |   | A |   |   |   |   |
| O | I |   | Y |   | K |   |   | H |
| Z |   | Y |   | I | S | L |   |   |
| S | O |   | H | L |   | K |   |   |
|   | H |   | O |   |   |   |   | S |

14

Part I: Texas People

## Stunt Doubles

The first and last names of 12 actors from Texas have been split into two-letter segments. The letters in each segment are in order, but the segments have been mixed up. Put together the pieces in each line to come up with the performers' names. Answers on page 139.

1. JO HA HN ES WK

2. TH YB AK KA ER

3. IN RT MA RY MA

4. MP SO JI AR NS

5. RA SA HS HI HA

6. ER MA HY RT HA

7. CR AW RD FO AN JO

8. RS RO ER GE GI NG

9. LE VA RI EP RI NE ER

10. BB RE OL DE IE YN DS

11. ER AK FO IT WH ST RE

12. NN JE ER IF RN GA ER

15

Texas Crosswords

# TV News Crossword
Solution on page 139.

### Across
1. "Tommy" rockers
7. Assn.
10. Norway's largest city
14. CBS Evening News anchor
15. "Say what?"
16. H-E-B Grocery price check
17. Release
18. Fukumoto Sushi sash
19. In vogue
20. I-20 horn sound

### Down
1. It's a fact
2. Vietnam's capital
3. Community spirit
4. One of five Ws for an Athens Daily Review reporter
5. East Poultry Company coop dweller
6. Big test
7. Dark Hour Haunted House resident

16

# Part I: Texas People

## Across (cont.)

21. Ford flop
23. Texas Senate assistant
24. ___ and hers
25. "Hold on!"
26. Harp's cousin
28. Rice athletes
29. Decatur Tire Store filler
30. Rx watchdog
33. Circle parts
36. Answers an invitation
38. Swell
39. Teen ___
40. Manages
41. Formally surrender
42. Texas interstate
43. Not rural
44. Fortuneteller's card
45. Gasteyer of Mean Girls
46. LSU, to Texas A&M
47. Liberty Power network
49. "Crazy" bird
51. Hammer's end
52. Diaper wearer
55. "High Voltage" band
57. Target rival
59. Vice president under Jefferson
60. Burst of wind
61. UT physics class study
62. Shoppe descriptor
64. Valley Symphony Orchestra woodwind
65. Numerical prefix
66. CBS Evening News anchor
67. Lady's escort
68. List abbr.
69. Senior members

## Down (cont.)

8. Country bumpkin
9. Dateline NBC anchor
10. Joan Crawford's prized statuette
11. CBS Evening News anchor
12. Set, as a trap
13. ___ and for all
22. Strip at Chicas Locas
25. It ended 11/11/18
27. Soph. and jr. at TCU
28. Texas tea
29. Superhero group member
31. Woodworking groove
32. Assist in crime
33. 2005 deadly hurricane
34. Gulf port
35. ABC's World News Sunday anchor
37. Ritz-Carlton amenity
40. CBS Evening News anchor
41. Scoundrel
43. ET's craft
44. Element #50 in a Cy-Fair HS science class
48. Enter data again
50. Santa's reindeer, e.g.
51. Lose one's cool
52. Gown fabric
53. Wharton County Court call
54. Rockets' three-point baskets
55. Awestruck
56. Rubik's ___
58. "Beetle Bailey" cartoonist Walker
59. Fearless
63. Aka Sushi House fish

## Musical Performers

A highlight of any trip to Austin is its live music scene. Texans and visitors alike flock to the city's numerous clubs and bars, particularly those on the bustling Sixth Street and South Congress Avenue. The state capital has more than 250 venues that feature all types of music, from country and rock to blues and jazz.

The city's South by Southwest (SXSW) festival is held every March and features musical performances as well as films and interactive media. Started in 1987, this festival is a huge event, attracting around 2,000 musical acts and nearly 30,000 attendees each year. President Barack Obama talked of ways the technology industry could help some of America's greatest problems at SXSW Interactive in 2016.

Austin City Limits is another Texas icon. This PBS show airs weekly and features musical performances. The premiere was in 1974 and featured Willie Nelson. Recent performers have included Ed Sheeran, Ben Harper, Alabama Shakes, and Robert Plant. The ACL Music Festival draws 450,000 attendees and is held each fall in Zilker Park. The festival has hosted huge acts, including the Dave Matthews Band, Widespread Panic, Drake, John Mayer, Jack Johnson, and Keith Urban.

For a unique experience, visitors head to Gruene in Texas Hill Country. This is where Texas's oldest dance hall, Gruene Hall, features live music every day. Built in 1878, this venue hosts up-and-coming stars, songwriters trying out new material, or superstars seeking an intimate environment. The quaint 6,000-square-foot building has a high pitched tin roof. There's a small stage, large outdoor garden, bar, and the chance for open-air dancing under the stars. John Travolta fans may remember the dance hall from his movie Michael.

Texas's rock 'n' roll history is strong, as it was the birthplace of 1950s superstars Buddy Holly (Lubbock) and Roy Orbison (Vernon and Wink). Holly is most known for "That'll be the Day," a song he wrote and sang with his band The Crickets. Tragically Holly's career was cut short when he died at age twenty-two in a plane crash.

Orbison, a singer, songwriter, and musician, saw twenty-two of his songs hit the Billboard Top Forty from 1960 to 1966. Some of his most popular hits were "Crying" and "Oh, Pretty Woman." "The Big O" revived his career in 1988 when he teamed with rock superstars Tom Petty, Bob Dylan, George Harrison, and Jeff Lynne to form the Traveling Wilburys. Orbison died later that year at age fifty-two.

Roy Orbison was born in Vernon, Texas and revolutionized the music industry, inspiring stars from Van Halen to Bruce Springsteen.

Texas Crosswords

# Country Music Crossword
Solution on page 139.

### Across

1. Dole (out)
5. Fastener
10. Ray Roberts Lake State Park unit: ____ du Bois
14. Singer of "Ten Rounds with Jose Cuervo"
15. Texas state highway, e.g.
16. Host of The Country Roads Show
17. Dallas Carpet Outlet calculation
18. Spud

### Down

1. UT bus. degrees
2. Bronte heroine
3. Masterson State Forest growth
4. Whole Foods Market cheese
5. PC component
6. Unwilling
7. Only person awarded stars in all five categories on the Hollywood Walk of Fame
8. Astros baserunner's ploy

20

# Part I: Texas People

## Across (cont.)

19. Prospector's find
20. Appears
22. Houston Methodist Hospital ER concern
24. Gas additive
26. National Videogame Museum name
30. Beaver, at times
34. Haberdashery Boutique item
35. "___ we forget"
36. Degraded
40. Part of TGIF
41. Arlington fraternal group
42. "King of Western Swing"
43. Blues singer Mayes
44. Beast of burden
45. Jazz trumpeter: Don ___
46. Rapper-turned-actor
47. SH 6 roadside stops
49. Texas Roadhouse diners
51. Texas Southern dorm annoyance
52. Phobias
55. Take away
57. Waste maker
62. University Hospital supplies
65. Lab gels
67. Texas legislative alliance
68. Recorder of What I Really Mean
69. African capital
70. "Country Caruso"
71. "Thanks ___!"
72. Cathedral Santuario de Guadalupe recesses
73. Rush Elementary School playground retort

## Down (cont.)

9. Cuzco's country
10. White Rabbit's cry
11. ___ Paulo
12. TV type
13. Barely get, with "out"
21. Get the picture
23. Overton Hotel worker
25. Fishes with a net at Lake Fork
27. For each
28. "Tex" whose son and grandsons became actors
29. Texas map blowups
30. Flashes
31. Named by Rolling Stone as one of the "100 Greatest Singers" and "100 Greatest Guitarists"
32. Invites out for
33. Lb. and kg.
34. Neiman Marcus perfume sampler
37. Eddie V's Prime Seafood lobster dinner accessory
38. Trinity Hall Irish Pub brew
39. Certain camera, for short
43. Franklin Barbecue hot spot
45. On the safe side, in the Gulf
48. Off-course
50. Rangers bat wood
52. Get all steamy
53. Born Lucille Wood Smith in Uvalde, Tex.
54. Fairfield Lake State Park eagle's home
56. ___ Hari (spy)
58. "Dancing Queen" group
59. Houston blight
60. Light throw by Dak Prescott
61. Airmen's Cave sound effect
62. Caribbean music
63. Matsu Sushi Bar fish
64. ___ Speedwagon
66. Gatlin's BBQ sound

# Texas Crosswords

## Buck Owens Sudoku

Use logic to fill in the boxes so every row, column and 3x3 box contains the letters B–U–C–K–O–W–E–N–S in honor of Buck Owens. The Sherman native had 21 No. 1 hits on the Billboard country music charts, but is best remembered for co-hosting the TV series Hee Haw. Solution on page 139.

| U |   | S |   |   |   |   |   | N |
|---|---|---|---|---|---|---|---|---|
|   | W |   | B |   |   |   | K |   |
|   |   |   |   | E |   |   |   | U |
|   |   |   | W |   | E |   | U |   |
|   |   | B |   |   |   | O |   |   |
|   | E |   | S |   | C |   |   |   |
| E |   |   |   | C |   |   |   |   |
|   | K |   |   |   | O |   | S |   |
| O |   |   |   |   |   | E |   | B |

## Joplin Sudoku

Use logic to fill in the grid so every row, column and 2x3 box contains the letters J–O–P–L–I–N, in honor of Janis Joplin. She was born in Port Arthur and became one of the most popular rock singers of the 1960s. She died of a heroin overdose at the age of 27. Solution on page 140.

|   |   | L | I |   |   |
|---|---|---|---|---|---|
| I | P |   |   | O |   |
|   |   |   |   | N | I |
| J | N |   |   |   |   |
|   | I |   |   | P | J |
|   |   | N | O |   |   |

Part I: Texas People

## Star Crossed

Place the letters at the bottom of each grid into the empty squares to form the first and last names of six musicians with Texas connections. Solutions of page 140.

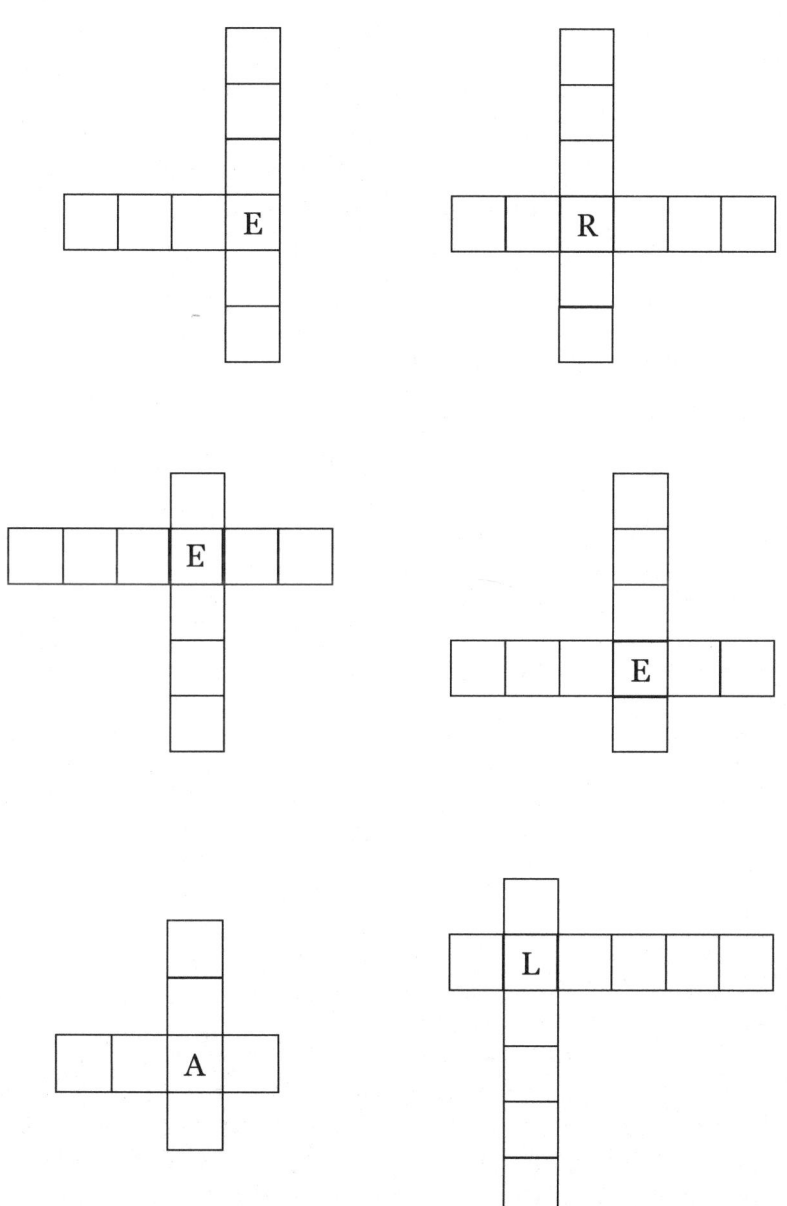

# Legendary Women

There is no shortage of amazing famous women from Texas. Some of the world's greatest athletes, singers, politicians and business women have called The Lone Star State home.

One of the greatest athletes of all time was Babe Didrikson Zaharias. Nicknamed "The Texas Tomboy" and "The Texas Babe," Zaharias grew up in Beaumont and succeeded in every sport she tried—and she tried a lot! In the 1932 Olympics, she qualified for five events. She played baseball as a child, and that's where she earned her nickname "Babe." Spectators thought she played like the famous Yankee Babe Ruth. In high school, Zaharias competed in baseball, basketball, golf, swimming, tennis and volleyball—all at a time when women's athletics were not well accepted. She eventually won thirty-one tournaments as a pro golfer. Even while battling cancer in 1954, she won her third US Women's Open in Golf and was named the Associated Press's Athlete of the Year (for the sixth time).

Two of America's most interesting entrepreneurs wrote their stories in Texas. Bette Nesmith Graham, a Dallas secretary, had a common problem—correcting messy typing mistakes. Graham figured that she could simply "paint" over her mistakes, leading her to invent a product she called "Mistake Out." Once the other secretaries found out about the invention, her product took off. She began manufacturing the paint—which she renamed "Liquid Paper"—at home. She was selling 40,000 bottles a week by 1968 and sold the company for $47.5 million in 1980.

Mary Kay Ash was the pink-loving founder of a multi-million dollar cosmetics company bearing her name, Mary Kay Cosmetics. When she became disillusioned at her sales job after being passed over for a promotion, Ash left the corporate world in 1963. She decided to write a book to help business women; that book became her business plan. After her husband George Hellenbeck passed away and with a $5,000 investment, Ash started Mary Kay Cosmetics in Dallas. The company

## Part I: Texas People

is still thriving today, with sales around $3.5 billion a year. Ash purchased the company's first pink Cadillac in 1968. Pink Cadillacs are synonymous with Mary Kay Cosmetics, as the company has rewarded its company's top salesperson with this vehicle for years.

Though she was not born in Texas, Georgia O'Keeffe may be one of the Lone Star State's greatest proponents. She taught in Amarillo's public schools, and in 1916, O'Keeffe joined West Texas State Normal College in Canyon. She taught art and headed the department. While there, she created at least fifty paintings, including "The Flag," an expression of her thoughts on World War I, and a series of watercolor paintings featuring the Palo Duro Canyon.

Courtesy of Carl Van Vechten via the Library of Congress

Georgia O'Keeffe is often called the Mother of American Modernism. Originally from Wisconsin, O'Keeffe taught at several schools in Texas, including the West Texas State Normal College.

# Women Crossword

Solution on page 140.

### Across

1. AT&T Stadium surface
5. Davy Crockett National Forest doe beau
9. Change the Constitution of Texas
14. Lone Star Fencing sword
15. Model linked to Mick Jagger and Rupert Murdoch
16. Co-founder of the largest private foundation in the US
17. Paint can direction
18. Icy coating

### Down

1. Trinity University final, e.g.
2. Until
3. Turkey Creek Stables bit attachment
4. Texas' first female governor
5. Rip to pieces
6. Word before chi or after mai
7. ___ mater
8. "Galveston" singer
9. Forever young

# Part I: Texas People

## Across (cont.)

19. Fund the Communities Foundation of Texas
20. Shoe part
22. Perspective
24. Culebra Meat Packing govt. overseer
26. "C'mon!"
30. "God ___ America"
33. Rationale
36. Blue Jays, on Globe Life Park scoreboards
37. Midtown Auto Service bill segment
38. Fuzz bits
39. King of France
40. Loads
41. Disney Channel actress-turned-pop star
42. Harris County Animal Control pen
43. ___ Speedwagon
44. Composed a story for the Weatherford Democrat
45. Con man's plant
46. Hill Country game ranch target
47. Bit of gossip
48. Hall's pop partner
49. Part of GPS
51. San Antonio hoopster
53. Backs of necks
56. Singer Newton-John
60. Brook Hollow Golf Club fairway chunk
63. KCBD weather radar dot
65. Religious subgroup
66. "The Grand Dame of Dish": Liz ___
67. Singer fined for appearing nude in a Dallas plaza while filming a music video
68. Jenny's Alterations line
69. Easy gaits at Four Bar K Ranch
70. Exchange
71. Coastal raptors

## Down (cont.)

10. Museum of Fine Arts impressionist
11. DFW info
12. Prefix with natal
13. Preston Center shoe store letters
21. Cold War inits.
23. Razzle-dazzle
25. Flowering
27. Shipping route
28. Search site
29. Prokop Custom Home bay windows
30. Austin traffic jam din
31. Nowadays
32. Kindle downloads
34. "We ___ please"
35. Nasty smiles
41. Crotchety sort
42. Hollywood dancer awarded the National Medal of the Arts and Humanities
44. The Galleria year-end decorations
45. Cactus Music genre
50. Fed. bond
52. Astros infield fly
54. Recedes
55. Gatlin's BBQ side
57. Zig or zag on I-10
58. Volunteer's offer
59. United Texas Bank offerings
60. ISP alternative
61. Texting qualifier
62. Texas Memorial Stadium suite guest
64. Bob Wills and his Texas Playboys: "___ Red"

# Texas Crosswords

## Jordan Sudoku

Use logic to fill in the grid so every row, column and 2x3 box contains the letters J–O–R–D–A–N, in honor of Barbara Jordan. The Houston native was a member of the U.S. House of Representatives and was the first African-American woman to deliver a keynote address at a Democratic National Convention. Solution on page 140.

| R |   | A | N |   | J |
|---|---|---|---|---|---|
|   |   |   |   |   |   |
| D |   | J | A |   |   |
|   |   | O | J |   | D |
|   |   |   |   |   |   |
| J |   | D | O |   | R |

## Dworaczyk Sudoku

Use logic to fill in the boxes so every row, column and 3x3 box contains the letters D–W–O–R–A–C–Z–Y–K, in honor of Hope Dworaczyk. The Miss Texas Teen USA-turned-model and reality TV star was born and raised at Port Lavaca. Solution on page 140.

|   |   |   |   | C | W |   | K |   |
|---|---|---|---|---|---|---|---|---|
| R |   |   |   | A | Z |   |   |   |
| C | O |   |   |   | Y | A | D |   |
| D |   |   | O |   | W |   | Z |   |
|   | Z |   |   | Y |   |   | K |   |
|   | K |   | A |   | R |   |   | W |
|   | D | Z | Y |   |   |   | W | C |
|   |   |   |   | Z | D |   |   | Y |
| Y |   | A |   | R |   |   |   |   |

28

Part I: Texas People

## Cryptic Quote

The Cryptic Quote is a substitution cipher in which one letter stands for another. If you think that A equals Z, it will equal Z throughout the puzzle. Solve this Cryptic Quote from Barbara Bush, the former First Lady and mother of a US President. (HINT: Every D here is actually an A.) Solution on page 140.

I Z X I S Z    N A X    N X C C L

D J X O M    M A Z T C    A D T C

D S S    M A Z    M T K Z,

G C D P R S L,    D C Z

J X C T P U.

# Texas Crosswords

## Politicians

Sometimes called the Founding Father of Texas, Sam Houston played many roles. He was a soldier, Texas's first (and third) president, a US senator, and Texas's governor. Houston was in command of forces in the Battle of San Jacinto, freeing Texas from Mexico. As governor, he was opposed to secession (rare for a state in the south) and refused to pledge allegiance to the Confederacy, for which he was removed from office. Texas's most populous city is, of course, named after Houston.

The Bush family name has become synonymous with Texas. George H. W. Bush was born in Massachusetts, but moved to Texas after serving in the US Navy during World War II, attending Yale, and marrying his wife, Barbara. He served in Congress, as director of the CIA, and as vice president before becoming the forty-first US president.

His son George W. was born in Connecticut in 1946. He followed in his father's footsteps, graduating from Yale and working in the oil industry. George W. married Laura in 1977. He became Texas governor in 1994 and the forty-third US president in 2000.

Dwight D. Eisenhower and Lyndon B. Johnson are two other presidents from Texas. Eisenhower was born in Denison, but did not live there long. Johnson, however, was the epitome of Texas. The thirty-sixth president (1963–69) was born in Stonewall. He was educated in Texas, attending college at what is now Texas State University in San Marcos. After graduation, he worked as a teacher. Johnson married "Lady Bird" Johnson in 1943.

Johnson served in the US House of Representatives and Senate before being name John F. Kennedy's vice president in 1960. After leaving the White House, the Johnsons went home to LBJ Ranch in Stonewall. The ranch is now a national historical park that includes his birthplace, home, ranch, and final resting place. His presidential library is on the Austin campus of the University of Texas.

One of the most groundbreaking women from Texas was civil rights activist Barbara Jordan. Jordan grew up in Houston's Fifth Ward

Part I: Texas People

where she attended Phillis Wheatley High School. She had hoped to attend UTA, but could not due to segregation. Instead she went to Texas Southern University, where she majored in political science and history and graduated *magna cum laude*. Jordan began her political career in the Texas Senate after attending Boston University's School of Law. In 1972, Jordan became the first black woman elected to the US Congress from a former Confederate state. She is often remembered for her strong speaking skills and the keynote address at the 1976 Democratic Convention. Jordan passed away in 1996 and became the first African-American woman to be buried in Austin's Texas State Cemetery, an honor reserved for Texas heroes.

Texas has had two female governors, the first of whom was Miriam Amanda Wallace "Ma" Ferguson. She served from 1925 to 1927 and 1933 to 1935. Her husband, James "Pa" Ferguson was governor from 1915 to 1917 but was impeached during this second term, which is when Ma entered the picture. During both her terms, Ferguson stood up against the Ku Klux Klan, implemented state sales and corporate income taxes, granted many pardons from prison, and stood with the "wets" during prohibition.

Texas's most recent female governor was Ann Richards, another Democrat. Richards was known for her wit, shining personality, and emphasis on education. She grew up in Waco and attended Baylor, where she had a debate team scholarship. She also attended UTA, where she received a teaching certificate. She took up politics on a whim after a career in teaching. She became the state treasurer before being elected governor in 1990.

Courtesy of Thomas O'Halloran via the Library of Congress

Lyndon B. Johnson, shown here as a senator in 1955, would later become America's 36th President following the assassination of JFK in 1963.

31

# Texas Crosswords

## Politicians Crossword

Solution on page 140.

### Across

1. Baylor frat letter
5. Storage spot
10. Moonshine vessel
13. US Senator of Cuban descent born in Canada
14. Clog clearer
15. A Beatle bride
16. In the know
17. Object of worship
18. "___ enough?"

### Down

1. Chilly attitude
2. "Annie" extras
3. Texas Ballet Theater attire
4. Portuguese islands
5. Do sums at Ortiz Elementary School
6. Pick up the tab at Firehouse Bar
7. Taiwan capital
8. Astros unpaid worker
9. Playing hard to get

Part I: Texas People

## Across (cont.)

19. OK
21. Houston Zoo beast
22. San Antonio-to-Abilene dir.
23. Mermaid's home
24. Spring time
26. Anthem start
28. QVC rival
29. Dine at Copper Creek
30. Still to come
32. Draft inits.
34. Braunfels lead-in
36. Small choir
37. First female US Senator from Texas
41. Chris Cooper's prized statuette
44. American Airlines pilot's problem
45. Ambulance letters
48. Soft fabric
51. Texas A&M school
53. Texas Electric Cooperatives unit
55. Video recorder
56. Carpentry tool
58. Antique auto
59. Platoon setting
60. UT's 2009 Fiesta Bowl foe
61. Type of thermometer
63. Woodworking tool
64. H-E-B Center gate
66. A-list
67. 2016 Olympics city
68. Battle of the Alamo, e.g.
69. GHW or GW
70. Mavs stats
71. Ace Hardware buy
72. Spots

## Down (cont.)

10. 36th US President
11. Out of it
12. Word on all US coins
16. "Pipe down!"
20. Razz the Red Raiders foe
22. Zero
25. Design detail
27. Thus far
31. ___-Cone
33. Hello and goodbye
35. Temple Daily Telegram reporter's question
38. Dot-com's address
39. Dog food brand
40. Curse
41. Needville Harvest Fest mo.
42. Bash
43. First Hispanic US Cabinet member
46. Tenon's partner
47. Sword cases
49. Like some humor
50. Beyonce, to Solange Knowles
52. Nerds
54. Dallas Pest Control target
57. Get rid of
62. Whodunit hint
63. Lubbock Animal Services bark
64. Twisty curve on SH 31
65. Fine-grained wood

## Who Am I? Sudoku

Here's another Sudoku with a twist. You still use logic to fill in the boxes so every row, column and 3x3 box contains the same nine letters. But when the puzzle is completed, the name of a man who was the governor, lieutenant governor and a state senator will be revealed in the line indicated by the arrow. Solution on page 140.

|   | L |   | A | T | K |   |   |   |
|---|---|---|---|---|---|---|---|---|
| T | O |   |   | S |   |   |   |   |
| D |   | K |   |   | O |   |   |   |
|   | E | A |   |   |   | D | K |   |
| ▶ |   |   |   |   |   |   |   |   |
| K | D |   |   | L | T |   |   |   |
|   | C |   |   | A |   |   |   | S |
|   |   | L |   |   |   | C | A |   |
|   | D | T | C |   | L |   |   |   |

▶ _____

## Austin Sudoku

Use logic to fill in the grid so every row, column and 2x3 box contains the letters A–U–S–T–I–N, in honor of Stephen F. Austin. Known as "The Father of Texas," Austin was the Secretary of State of Texas at the time of his death. Solution on page 141.

|   | U | T |   |   |   |
|---|---|---|---|---|---|
|   |   | S | N |   |   |
|   |   | U | S |   | N |
| I |   | N | U |   |   |
|   |   | I | A |   |   |
|   |   |   | T | U |   |

Part I: Texas People

## Senators Word Search

Solution on page 141.

```
B M I L L S K Y G F E T D B V
L Q Y J T O W E R Z K W E Y W
Y C B K R U E G E R O K R C Q
D E H T H V E H J W C C R U Z
L N L I B G C W S Q O D N B P
D O N I L V U I F N C O V E Y
L S E N A T B O N O T D M R E
E I S J K B O A R S Z M V S X
I H T O L P L N U O A L N O A
F C N H E L Y O M R B U A N M
Y T E N Y N H R G Z F R G F U
A U B S J N O S N H O J A M V
M H G T F L A N A G A N E Y X
Q U D O D A N I E L F F R R T
A I S N S H E P P A R D C G V
```

| | | |
|---|---|---|
| BAILEY | CUBERSON | KRUEGER |
| BENTSEN | DANIEL | MAXEY |
| BLAKLEY | FLANAGAN | MAYFIELD |
| CHILTON | GRAMM | MILLS |
| COKE | HOUSTON | REAGAN |
| CONNALLY | HUTCHISON | SHEPPARD |
| CORNYN | JOHNSON | TOWER |
| CRUZ | JOHNSTON | YARBOROUGH |

# Writers

Peruse any list of famous writers and Texas will be well represented. The state has produced stellar writers in all genres—from literature to poetry to journalism.

Molly Ivins fit in that latter category. Raised in Houston, Ivins worked at several Texas newspapers before becoming a syndicated columnist. Ivins worked on her high school newspaper and yearbook staffs at St. Johns School and attended Smith College and the Columbia University Graduate School of Journalism. She started as a police reporter at the *Minneapolis Tribune* before moving on to the *Texas Observer*, the *New York Times*, the *Dallas Time Herald*, and the *Fort Worth Star-Telegram*. The Austin-based Ivins had a humorous point of view and loved to use it to write about politics. Her syndicated column was carried in hundreds of US newspapers.

The Lone Star State served as the backdrop for many of Larry McMurtry's works. This author has seen many of his books become successful, award-winning movies, including *The Last Picture Show* and *Terms of Endearment*. The author, who was born in Archer City and grew up on a Texas ranch, was an avid reader as a child. He attended the University of North Texas and Rice University. McMurtry won a Pulitzer Prize for his novel *Lonesome Dove*, which later became a TV miniseries. He wrote several other books in this series which also made it to TV. McMurtry won an Academy Award (Best Adapted Screenplay) with his cowriter Diana Ossana of *Brokeback Mountain*.

Though not a native Texan, James Michener may be one of the state's most beloved authors. In his later life, Michener and his wife Mari settled in Austin. The couple donated $37 million to UTA, making them the school's largest single donor at the time (1992). They endowed the Michener Center for Writers there. This center offers Michener Fellowships in fiction, poetry, playwriting, and screenwriting.

Part I: Texas People

Michener focused on mainly lengthy historical fiction books. He wrote about generations of families in various geographic locales. He won the Pulitzer Prize for *Tales of the South Pacific* in 1948. Other popular novels included Hawaii, *The Drifters* and *Centennial. South Pacific* was his first book adapted as a Broadway musical.

Others writers from Texas include O. Henry, Ted Dekker, Roy Bedichek, J. Frank Dobie, Cormac McCarthy, and Max Lucado.

Courtesy of Thomas J. O'Halloran via the Library of Congress

James A. Michener depicted here in 1977 was one of the best-selling authors of the twentieth century. He is perhaps best known for his historical fiction including *Texas*, which is still in print today.

## Authors Crossword

Solution on page 141.

### Across

1. UT thespian's major
6. Texas Reptile Zoo critter, briefly
10. Galveston beachcombers concern
14. Katmandu's land
15. Gov. Abbott swearing-in words
16. "I had no ___!"
17. Pick a pet at Prairie Paws
18. Tiny bit
19. Cheery tune

### Down

1. DPD forensic evidence
2. Texas Tech ___ Raiders
3. GI's address
4. Pancake House syrup flavor
5. Lubbock Chorale voice
6. Snap out of it
7. Texas Card House poker ploy
8. The Simpsons bus driver
9. SMU lab course
10. Spanish squiggle

Part I: Texas People

## Across (cont.)

20. Pulitzer Prize-winning novel by 38-Across
23. Prosperity Bank quote
26. Western Indian
27. Mideast land
28. Naval off.
29. Lennon's lady
30. Jason's Deli bread
32. The French Room goodbye
34. Klein HS sci. class
35. Appropriate
38. Author of 20- and 56-Across
42. Tyler Morning Telegraph VIPs
43. Cowboys punt path
44. Lands heavily
46. Glide over Lake Conroe
47. American Airlines Center's Kiss ____
49. Came in first in the AL West
50. Code name
54. Red, Hot & Blue Festival fireworks cry
55. In addition
56. Novel by 38-Across
60. Surfing need
61. After-lunch sandwich
62. Spohn Hospital sign of life
66. Turner's Gardenland buy
67. Texas flag feature
68. Lip shine
69. Rack Daddy's table cloth
70. Mailed
71. Do penance

## Down (cont.)

11. Manner of speaking
12. Dig (into)
13. No longer on the plate at Rooster's Roadhouse
21. St. Mark Catholic Church lady
22. Hurricane Harvey center
23. Electronics giant
24. Befuddle
25. Threesome
29. Willie Nelson: "____ Chain Of Love"
30. Toyota Center backboard attachment
31. TCU map phrase: "____ are here"
33. CHRISTUS Health areas
34. Secretive email option
35. Falcons, on NRG Stadium scoreboards
36. Search stealthily
37. The Brownsville Herald printing goofs
39. Talk, talk, talk
40. University Hospital pic
41. San Antonio Raceway tach stat
45. ____-Cat
46. Watery expanse
47. Associate
48. Shogun Sushi tuna
50. Workweek letters
51. Hobby destination in Chicago
52. Live it up
53. Unwelcome winter forecast
54. Porthole view
55. Six Flags ticket category
57. Jettison
58. One-named Deco artist found at Austin Galleries
59. Texas Classic links org.
63. Lav of London
64. xxx-xx-xxxx fig.
65. Language suffix

39

Texas Crosswords

## Howard Sudoku

Use logic to fill in the grid so every row, column and 2x3 box contains the letters H–O–W–A–R–D, in honor of Robert E. Howard. He spent most of his life in Cross Plains and wrote pulp fiction and is regarded as the father of the sword and sorcery subgenre. He created the character Conan the Barbarian. Solution on page 141.

|   |   |   |   |   |   |
|---|---|---|---|---|---|
| O |   |   |   |   |   |
|   | R | W | D |   | A |
| W |   | D | A |   |   |
|   |   | O | W |   | H |
| D |   | H | O | A |   |
|   |   |   |   |   | D |

## Title Box

Sandra Brown was born in Waco, grew up in Fort Worth and graduated from TCU. She is best known for her romance novels and thriller suspense books. She has used various pen names, including "Rachel Ryan." The box of letters below contains the title of one of her early romantic novels. Starting with the large L in the shaded box, move one square up, down, left or right (but not diagonally) and continue to move that way to spell out the title. The book's name runs continuously and uses each letter in the grid exactly once. Solutino on page 141.

| Y | E | B | N |
|---|---|---|---|
| O | *L* | E | O |
| N | O | V | S |
| D | R | E | A |

Part I: Texas People

## What's in a Name?

An anagram is a word, phrase or sentence formed by rearranging all the letters of another word, phrase or sentence. For example, an anagram for the name of Fort Worth writer BUD SHRAKE is BAD HUSKER. Now match these anagrams with the Texas writers listed. Answers on page 141.

1. NARROW BANDS
2. CHEEKIER ENTRANT
3. RABBI HOME DECOR
4. RISK FROM SEANCES
5. PEANUT PATROLS
6. SOME JEAN REARS
7. MOM TIPS JOHN
8. COOING ROOSTERS
9. VINYL LIMOS
10. CENTRAL PRIZE

a. Sandra Brown
b. Liz Carpenter
c. Katherine Center
d. Deborah Crombie
e. Molly Ivins
f. Frances Mossiker
g. Paul Patterson
h. James Reasoner
i. Jim Thompson
j. Sergio Troncoso

BONUS: Now it's your turn. See if you can create an anagram for FRED GIPSON (the author of Old Yeller). There are no wrong answers. Our two-word anagram involves a college art teacher, but you might come up with something else.

# Business

Texas's business was built on its land—cattle, cotton, lumber, and oil. While these industries continue today, the state is now a leader in technology and tourism as well. The Texas economy is the second largest in the nation.

In 1901, Engineer Anthony F. Lucas drilled Texas's first major oil well at Spindletop, near Beaumont. Refineries followed and the largest oil refinery in the contiguous US, the East Texas Oil Field, was discovered in 1930. ExxonMobil is the largest of the Big Oil companies. With its headquarters in Irving, this company is the world's largest publicly traded international oil and gas company. Phillips 66 and Valero are two other Fortune 500 oil companies located in Texas, Houston and San Antonio respectively.

Cotton was first grown in Texas by Spanish missionaries in the 1700s. Today, Texas leads the US in cotton production, making up about 40% of the country's crop—at a value of about $2.1 billion—each year. But climate change is putting this crop—and Texas's cattle industry—in jeopardy. Recent droughts have hurt nearly all Texas crops and have caused some ranches and businesses to close or lay off workers.

Ever since the first integrated circuit was first developed in Dallas, Texas has been a hotbed activity in the technology industry. Jack Kilby was the Texas Instruments employee who started it all in 1958. TI is still designing and manufacturing semiconductors and various integrated circuits today, with its headquarters in Dallas. Dell Technologies (Round Rock) and AT&T (Dallas) are two other Texas Fortune 500 companies.

H-E-B Grocery Company is based in San Antonio, Texas. Through its hunger relief program, H-E-B has donated more than 1 billion pounds of food.

Part I: Texas People

## Business Fill-in

Fill in the missing letter for each of the words listed. Be careful, because all of the words can be completed with more than one letter. Transfer the correct letter to the corresponding line so that the result is the name of a Plano-based business. Answer on page 141.

___  ___  ___  ___  ___      ___  ___  ___
 1    2    3    4    5        6    7    8

1. __ A R M
2. W A __ D
3. L __ N E
4. P U N __
5. C __ M E
6. __ A K E
7. L __ R D
8. B U R __

## Drop Down Quote

The letters in each vertical column in the grid below go into the squares directly above them, but not necessarily in the order they appear. The black squares indicate the end of a word. (Words can continue from the end of each line to the start of the next line.) When you have placed all the letters in their correct positions, you will have a quotation reading from left to right, row by row, from Humble-native Howard Hughes, one of the richest men in the world in the 1950s and '60s. Solution on page 141.

| E | I | E | E | C | E | E | A | C | O | H | A | D | G | H | I | S |
|---|---|---|---|---|---|---|---|---|---|---|---|---|---|---|---|---|
| E | P | I | I | T | M | M |   | N | R | U | A | S | N | U | T |   |
| L | V | K | R | Y |   |   |   | O |   | R | L |   |   |   | Y |   |
|   | X | R | S |   |   |   |   |   |   |   |   |   |   |   |   |   |

43

# Texas Crosswords

## Industrialists Crossword

Solution on page 141.

### Across

1. ___ John's Pizza
5. Dallas Table Tennis Club shot
10. Highlander
14. Computer maven named "Entrepreneur of the Year" by Inc. at age 24
15. Gung-ho
16. Boat in Jaws
17. Gift tag word
18. Aligns

### Down

1. Some emailed files
2. Sleek, for short
3. Clever tactic
4. "___ for the poor"
5. HPD sting operation
6. Co-founder of a department store that bears his name
7. Fever and chills
8. Envision

## Part I: Texas People

### Across (cont.)

19. J Five Horse Ranch newborn
20. Matsu Sushi Bar staple
22. Reef ring
23. PC brain
24. Cosmetics queen
26. Texas golfer with a career Grand Slam
30. Expertise
32. Briefs, e.g.
34. Hodgepodge
35. SHSU prof's aides
38. "Number theorist"/banker worth $11.6 billion
39. Founder of EDS who ran for US President
41. Businessman who is in the Pro Football, National Soccer and International Tennis halls of fame
42. "You don't ___"
43. Move slowly
44. Has a loan from Wells Fargo
46. Congregation Beth Israel scroll
48. Out of whack
49. Former CEO of HP known as Carly
53. Final (Abbr.)
55. Jim Parsons TV awards
56. Worked up
61. Caprock Laundry unit
62. Some SMU students
64. Skirmish
65. Fiddle with a fiddle
66. Net worth component for Richard Kinder
67. Real estate mogul who bequeathed his fortune to start a university in Houston
68. Mix a drink at Bar Louie
69. Anna Nicole Smith jeans brand
70. ___ and aahs

9. Rangers slugger's stats

### Down (cont.)

10. Bighearted sort
11. Wynne state prison swindler
12. Florida horse-breeding city
13. Figure on a Clear Lake Bridge Club score sheet
21. Hastings HS breakout
22. A Guthrie
24. Cat pal of 43-Down
25. O'Connor successor
26. DFW, HOU and others
27. ___ Day vitamins
28. Aussie greeting
29. Be sick
31. 2018 Winter Olympics site
33. Flatware piece
35. Hogs Wild boar's head feature
36. Post Oak Poker Club buy-in
37. Pack away
40. Orchestra conductor Rachlin
41. Guys
43. Canine pal of 24-Down
45. Light bulb unit
47. Recluse who made a fortune in the aviation industry
49. Buffalo Billiards table surfaces
50. Prime Social Poker Club declaration
51. Saudi neighbor
52. U-Haul rival
54. Leans in the Gulf of Mexico
56. Corpus Christi Cathedral recess
57. Rich Jones ABA 'do
58. Los Lonely Boys, e.g.
59. Apiece
60. Harmony Hair Salon assortment
62. Droop
63. Big 12 sch.

Texas Crosswords

# Businesses Crossword

Solution on page 142.

## Across

1. Talk back to
5. East Dallas Knitting supply
9. Word on a TSP wanted poster
14. Off the Court author
15. El Paso Opera solo
16. Understood
17. San Antonio-based insurance company for veterans
18. San Antonio-based supermarket chain

## Down

1. Club Dallas hot spots
2. Per se
3. Soda bottled in Houston
4. Where to see buoys and gulls
5. Google rival
6. Range ridges
7. Killen's Barbecue staple
8. Hound
9. Discordant

# Part I: Texas People

## Across (cont.)

20. Some UT frat men
21. Preschoolers
22. Number of stars on a Texas flag
23. Perform with the Island East-End Theatre Company
24. "___ is me!"
25. Elate
29. Puppeteer Lewis
31. Skeleton topper in a Baylor anatomy class
33. "___ to Billie Joe"
34. Poet's planet
36. Word often shortened to its middle letter in texts
37. Margaret Mitchell classic, initially
38. Houston-based oilfield service company
41. Changed the locks at Headrush Salon
43. Sean ___ Lennon
44. "Dear" one
45. King of France
46. Tamron Hall's ex-news net.
48. Gift of the Magi
52. Outdo
54. Japanese PM
56. Mer contents
57. It may need massaging
58. Concluded
59. Houston Dash zero
60. Irving-based oil and gas corporation
64. Round Rock-based computer technology company
65. Sierra ___
66. Lab vessel
67. Curved molding
68. Decorate a cake at Sweets by Selina
69. Gillette brand
70. Comic-Con attendee, maybe

## Down (cont.)

10. Spiked the punch at a Denton HS dance
11. Dallas Stars playing surface
12. Put on KDFW
13. Farm area
19. Padre Island Hair Salon supplies
21. Coppell HS band majorette's move
25. Wise guy
26. Williams Tower elevator button
27. An hour ahead of CDT
28. Word before Fairview and Home in a Texas atlas
30. Line on an Austin map
32. Simply Greek menu item
35. Flourish
37. Like Texas Chainsaw Massacre
38. Next in line
39. Hill Country B&Bs
40. Texas Relays official
41. Seton Medical Center VIPs
42. "___ first!"
46. Fridge sticker
47. Roka Akor fish delicacy
49. Weasel out
50. Bitter critic
51. Out of the shell
53. Lowly workers
55. Twilight heroine
58. Sweetwater Reporter story of a lifetime
60. Santa's helper
61. Gen ___
62. Tic-tac-toe loser
63. Texas Fertility Center eggs
64. The Eagles' Henley

Texas Crosswords

## Companies Word Search
Solution on page 142.

```
L C I N E M A R K N H Q R S G
E G A U W H O L E F O O D S O
T F R I T O L A Y R D C Z Y G
I T R O C E L A N E S E L N T
H P B D G J N T P C O R F A I
C O K S R S I C I C R Y H O C
R T G E M E Q A G J Q P C R S
A S J P V M P R T L S S V I I
R E K N I R B P T N Y A L V R
O M J F K Z E E E S A I Q A A
E A W H R W Z S B P H U A L N
A G V O E D O A W C R K Q E E
V A U V U B E E H O F D H R T
I L S M Q Y C L Y U L F W O E
F Y L U Q R I J L B T F Q T B
```

| | | |
|---|---|---|
| ALCON | CITGO | KBR |
| ARCHITEL | DELL | PIZZA HUT |
| ASPYR | DR PEPPER | QUANTA |
| BRINKER | FLOWSERVE | SYSCO |
| CELANESE | FLUOR | TENARIS |
| CHILIS | FRITOLAY | USAA |
| CICIS | GAMESTOP | VALERO |
| CINEMARK | HEB | WHOLE FOODS |

Part I: Texas People

# Sports

As anyone who has ever watched Friday Night Lights can tell you, Texas is a football state. It doesn't matter whether it is high school, college, or pro—Texas has it all.

The Dallas Cowboys are "America's Team." They've been to the Super Bowl eight times and have won five. They play in Arlington at AT&T Stadium—the NFL's first billion-dollar stadium. The Houston Texans were founded in 2002, making them the league's youngest team. They play in NRG Stadium—the first venue in the NFL with a retractable roof. One of the Texans's most popular players is defensive end J. J. Watt, who helped raise $41.6 million for Hurricane Harvey relief.

In terms of college athletics, the Texas Longhorns play in Texas Memorial Stadium in Austin. The stadium holds more than 100,000, but is not as big as Kyle Field in College Station. The Texas A&M Aggies play in a stadium that seats 102,512. Other Division One football teams are Baylor, TCU, Tech Tech, SMU, Houston, North Texas, Rice, UTEP, UTSA, and Texas State.

Of course football is not Texas' only game. The state is home to two professional baseball teams. The Houston Astros won the World Series in 2017—their first title since the team was founded in 1962. The Rangers, based in Arlington, have won several AL West Division titles.

The NBA is well represented by the Dallas Mavericks, Houston Rockets, and San Antonio Spurs. The Mavericks are owned by controversial billionaire Mark Cuban. The Mavericks won the 2011 NBA Championship. The Rockets, led by University of Houston product Hakeem Olajuwon, won back-to-back NBA titles in 1994 and 1995. Texas's most successful team is the Spurs. This team has won five champions—in 1999, 2003, 2005, 2007 and 2014—and Tim Duncan was part of them all. Duncan is often called the greatest power forward of all time.

Texas's only professional hockey team, the Dallas Stars, has been in the NHL since 1993.

# Texas Crosswords

Texans also enjoy going to the rodeo, of course. With tie-down roping, bareback riding, bull riding, steer wrestling, barrel racing, and more, a rodeo is quite the spectacle. The world's largest rodeo is held each year in Houston—the Houston Livestock Show and Rodeo. The rodeo is nearly twenty weeks long; it drew a record-high crowd of 2,611,176 people in 2017.

The Lone Star State has produced its fair share of excellent athletes, including one of the best ever, Beaumont's Babe Didrikson Zaharias. Another superb Texas golfer was Ben Hogan, a four-time PGA Player of Year. The Fort Worth native is one of only four men to have won all four majors, including four US Opens. Another Fort Worther, Bryon Nelson, was a two-time Masters champ who won 11 straight tournaments in 1945. Jordan Spieth is the latest Texan star. In 2015, the Dallas native became the second-youngest golfer to win the Masters. He started playing golf at an early age at Dallas's Brookhaven Country Club.

Texas has been home to football players galore, including Doak Walker, Sammy Baugh, Earl Campbell, Y. A. Tittle, Eric Dickerson, "Mean" Joe Greene, and Tom Landry. Baseball stars Rogers Hornsby, Nolan Ryan, and Ernie Banks are Texas, as are boxers George Foreman and Jack Johnson. Other top athletes include A. J. Foyt (racing), Michael Johnson (track and field), and Sheryl Swoopes (basketball).

As the largest livestock exhibition and rodeo in the world, the Houston Livestock Show and Rodeo is viewed as teh city's signature event, on the same level as Mardi Gras in New Orleans or the Texas State Fair in Dallas.

Part I: Texas People

## Knight Moves

Bob Knight was head basketball coach at Texas Tech from 2001-08. In honor of the Hall of Fame Coach Knight, on a standard 8x8 chessboard, move from square to square the way a knight moves (between opposite corners of a 2x3 rectangle) to spell the names of 11 Texas Tech basketball stars (spanning more than just the Knight years), in alphabetical order. Begin at the big bold B in the top row (for the first letter in BATTIE). Now move like a knight and find an A (for the second letter in BATTIE). From there, move again as a knight to a T, and so on. Here's the tricky part: Do not use any letter on the board more than once. There are 64 letters in the players' names and 64 squares on the board, so each and every square should be used once. Solution on page 142.

| E | S | N | **B** | L | A | T | E |
|---|---|---|---|---|---|---|---|
| R | A | R | A | E | R | O | C |
| S | M | T | E | R | T | S | S |
| T | E | S | M | S | N | K | F |
| K | I | N | E | O | L | G | O |
| E | O | S | U | N | C | N | E |
| E | C | D | N | O | J | L | N |
| R | J | B | A | L | I | M | S |

BATTIE
BULLOCK   EMMETT    JACKSON   NOLEN    ROSS
CARR      FLEMONS   JENNINGS  REED     SASSER

Texas Crosswords

# Athletes Crossword

Solution on page 142.

### Across
1. Approximately
5. Ships
10. Practice for the Texas Golden Gloves
14. Four-time Indy 500 winner
15. Heavenly hunter
16. Part of HOMES
17. Type of type
18. ____ New Guinea

### Down
1. Counterbalance
2. Park Lane Guest House tenant
3. Genuine, for real
4. "Beetle Bailey" dog
5. Last year's Texas Tech frosh
6. Cleared
7. Barely beat the Owls
8. More like paste
9. Critter Control trap

## Part I: Texas People

### Across (cont.)

19. Community Bible Church prayer start
20. Makes level
22. RGIII
24. Wendy Barker's poetic nightfall
25. "It's no ___!"
26. Texas Chicken Coops layer
27. Winstead Law Firm charge
28. Secret meeting
30. 502, in old Rome
32. Snappy Salads green
34. State of mind
36. Lead-in to Boston and London in Texas
38. Table scraps
39. Cyclist stripped of seven Tour de France wins
42. Sir's partner
45. TiVo precursor
46. Put aside
48. Golfer Palmer, to pals
50. Charged particle in a Dobie HS science class
52. Set of principles
55. Droop
56. UT frat letters
58. Chicago destination from DFW
60. Zydeco musician: Queen ___
61. Seven-time Cy Young Award winner
63. Does a repair at Austin Shoe Hospital
65. 1952 Olympics host
66. Pause cause
68. Mattress Firm support
69. Boot Ranch Golf Club pegs
70. 17-Across choice
71. NBA all-star who was the son of an NFL all-pro
72. Back talk
73. New Light Christian Church song
74. St. Anthony Cathedral area

### Down (cont.)

10. Narcissist's love
11. Make a proposal
12. Most breezy
13. Sign of a rash
21. Texas State Writing Center coach
23. Snapple Group bus. card abbr.
29. "Me too"
31. Baylor textbook start
33. Thesaurus man
35. Texas licensing org.
37. China Inn skillet
40. Allure Hair Salon snippers
41. Has to have
42. Orbit and The Coyote
43. Asian body of water
44. Los ___
47. Ex-Cowboys running back Tanner
49. Odessa-to-Plano dir.
51. Standard
53. Worthy principles
54. Galveston beach creation
57. Open, as a bottle
59. Domain
62. Angelina National Forest growth
64. Dept. of Labor arm
67. "Mamma ___!"

Texas Crosswords

## A. J. Foyt Sudoku

Use logic to fill in the grid so every row, column and 2x3 box contains the letters A–J–F–O–Y–T, in honor of A. J. Foyt. The auto racer from Houston is the only driver to win the Indianapolis 500, Daytona 500, the 24 Hours of Daytona and the 24 Hours of Le Mans. Solution on page 142.

|   |   | J | T | A |   |
|---|---|---|---|---|---|
| A | F | O |   |   |   |
|   |   | Y |   |   |   |
|   |   |   | Y |   |   |
|   |   |   | T | J | O |
|   |   | J | O | A |   |

## Dez Bryant Sudoku

Use logic to fill in the boxes so every row, column and 3x3 box contains the letters D–E–Z–B–R–Y–A–N–T, in honor of Dez Bryant. He was born in Galveston County and grew up in Lufkin. He became a first round draft pick of the Dallas Cowboys in 2010 and has been a three-time Pro Bowl wide receiver. Solution on page 142.

|   | D |   |   |   | Y | N |   |   |
|---|---|---|---|---|---|---|---|---|
|   | B |   |   |   |   |   | A | E |
| N |   | A | R |   |   | Z |   |   |
| Z |   |   |   | D |   | Y |   |   |
|   |   |   | T |   | B |   |   |   |
|   |   |   | N |   | R |   |   | D |
|   |   | R |   |   | A | B |   | N |
| A | Y |   |   |   |   |   | D |   |
|   |   |   | E | Z |   |   | R |   |

Part I: Texas People

# Dallas Cowboys Word Search
Solution on page 143.

```
K S L R E V W Q H O D X J N S
Q L K T G O K T N X S F N O N
Y L D H U A I K M A N W A T I
N A O G Y M Y E L A H H D S K
W W R I S C M E T I X T R N R
L B S R Y W I T T E N I O H E
I U E W X N V E M F Q D J O P
L L T T O C S E R P L E Z J J
L S T A U B A C H S K R Q V S
Y Y I H F O J O R F N E R X R
P E A R S O N A A J M M T H E
N N I V R I X L H I H A A A D
U U L Y D A F L H O W L E Y N
E S D A E A H E I R K F J E A
F W O O D S O N Y H G O S S S
```

| AIKMAN | JOHNSTON | SANDERS |
| --- | --- | --- |
| ALLEN | JORDAN | SMITH |
| DORSETT | LILLY | STAUBACH |
| HALEY | MEREDITH | WALLS |
| HARRIS | PEARSON | WHITE |
| HAYES | PERKINS | WITTEN |
| HOWLEY | PRESCOTT | WOODSON |
| IRVIN | RENFRO | WRIGHT |

Texas Crosswords

# Sports Crossword
## Solution on page 143.

### Across
1. Ranch visitor
5. Salk's conquest
10. Do another hitch with the Texas National Guard
14. Ben Bridge Jeweler gem
15. Only major pro sports team in San Antonio's history
16. Abbey section
17. "____ It Romantic?"
18. Rope fiber

### Down
1. "Nothing ____!"
2. Open
3. MLS team named for Houston's energy-based industrial economy
4. Dell bus. card abbr.
5. Call to attention
6. Narcotic
7. Hungers (for)
8. Chase Bank offering
9. Capital near the 60th parallel

56

# Part I: Texas People

## Across (cont.)

19. Ashiana Indian Restaurant bread
20. PBS benefactor
21. Mavs fig.
22. Texter's "Holy cow!"
24. UT sorority letter
26. "For shame!"
28. 1965 King arrest site
32. Wyndam Hotel area
34. Facing a jury in Smith County Court
36. Hair Sensations supply
37. 15-Across original leag.
38. Deane's Boots Repair part
39. Haw partner
42. Team that plays in Houston's Toyota Center
45. Gov. Abbott veto
46. Oil cartel
48. Cable inits.
49. When repeated, a Latin dance
51. Sorrento Ristorante Italiano rice dish
53. Like some Texas A&M Singing Cadets music
56. Pronunciation symbol
57. Eavesdropping org.
59. Cushy class at TCU
61. AC stat
63. Starplex Pavilion concert gear
65. Maguire's Restaurant kitchen meas.
66. "So long!"
69. NorthPark Center shopping binge
71. Jack-o'-lantern feature
72. "I'm ___ human"
73. Only NHL team in Texas
74. Corn bread
75. KDBC Jag spin-off
76. Rushed
77. Fishing, perhaps

## Down (cont.)

10. Arlington team originally called the Senators
11. Clean air grp.
12. Red-white-and-blue inits.
13. Retirement gift from Shell, maybe
21. Not so crazy
23. One hr. behind CST
25. HPD photo
27. Lakers legend Bryant
29. Capital of Texas Zoo roarer
30. Timbuktu's land
31. Trading Spaces' McLeod
33. Be a bad winner
35. "Of course!"
37. Texas Tri-City Obedience org.
39. ___ d'oeuvre
40. Beowulf, e.g.
41. Fit together
43. "Let's go!"
44. Rack Room ___
47. Team with the colors Navy Blue, Metallic Silver, White and Royal Blue
50. Coach Parseghian
52. Artistic Encounter body art, briefly
53. KDFW news crew need
54. Team that won its first World Series in 2017
55. An amino acid
58. Kitchen wrap
60. Dallas Center for Sleep Disorders study
62. "Back in the ___"
64. Orkin target
66. Beaumont Federal Prison occupant
67. Co. name ender
68. "Rope-a-dope" boxer
70. Austin Middle School grp.
71. SMU transcript fig.

Texas Crosswords

## Texas Athletes Hodgepodge

Find names of all-time great Texas stars in the categories listed, going up, down, sideways, backwards or diagonally in the letter grid. No letter is used more than once. When you have found all 21 names, there will be 43 unused letters. Start at the top of the grid, move from left to right and work down row by row, filling in the spaces provided with the unused letters to spell a hidden name. Solution on page 143.

```
                        C
                    O   A   A
                I   C   M   L   S
            G   E   B   P   T   T   S
        G   D   A   B   B   U   A   I   L
    I   E   E   D   I   E   V   U   B   A   L
B   N   D   R   I   K   L   E   B   O   Y   I   F
O   Y   O   C   C   M   L   S   A   N   N   L   O
N   N   A   M   K   R   E   B   C   O   E   L   R
S   O   G   E   R   V   I   N   H   N   Z   Y   E
T   P   S   P   A   T   T   E   R   S   O   N   M
G   T   R   R   N   O   S   N   I   B   O   R   A
S   I   E   I   E   E   L   L   I   O   T   T   N
    W   L   S   N   D   N   A   M   K   I   A
        O   M   R   G   N   A   H   A   R
            O   O   O   E   E   I   A
                P   R   D   R   H
                    E   E   S
                        S
```

| AIKMAN | DORSETT | HENDERSON | PATTERSON |
| ALTUVE | ELLIOTT | LAYNE | ROBINSON |
| BERKMAN | FOREMAN | LILLY | SPRINGER |
| BIGGIO | GERVIN | MCCOY | STAUBACH |
| CAMPBELL | GILMORE | NOBIS | SWOOPES |
| CEDENO | | | |

58

Part I: Texas People

6 Cowboys Pro Bowlers

_____
_____
_____
_____
_____
_____

4 Longhorns All-Americans

_____
_____
_____
_____

3 Spurs Hall of Famers

5 Astros All-Stars

_____
_____
_____
_____
_____

_____
_____
_____

2 Olympic Gold Medalists

_____
_____

1 Heavyweight Boxing Champ

_____

Hidden Name:

_ _ _ _  _ _ _ _ _ _

_ _ _ _ _ _ _

59

Texas Crosswords

# Texas Rangers Word Search

Solution on page 143.

```
C N E G A H N E V E L K C V M N G T
L X K L M X T K F G C J P Y C N S X
L I S S J D W P T G H R D D D B I P
L S K O O R B X I E A I S S O A U Y
A D M C N E L L Y G G E N K N Y U F
H E R Z E U L Q O T H V A F A L X C
B T C L S E W N M G F R M C L O X G
H H B A T S Z L U R S W K R D R N F
S G G T L A E H G T V F C Y I O G O
R I O J U L H L A S L S I U R U Y R
A R N L M G A A D Y E M H T Q E F D
M W L O C L F W M D S L S U F N O E
W A V R T R Y N R E I M P F U H F Y
S T U L Q R O S S O R R U O E T L T
N I T S U A U W Q A G G I R E Q B X
Q W A L K E R B D D N E T A L P U D
M C C U L L O C H E T Y R O D M F N
R A S I R C L W H N R Y C S I T Z G
```

| | | | |
|---|---|---|---|
| ARMSTRONG | FORD | HICKMAN | MCNELLY |
| ATEN | GILLETT | HUGHES | PEOPLES |
| AUSTIN | GONZAULLAS | JONES | RIDDLES |
| BAYLOR | GUFFEY | KLEVENHAGEN | ROGERS |
| BROOKS | HALL | MARSH | ROSS |
| BURTON | HAMER | MCCULLOCH | WALKER |
| CROWDER | HAYS | MCDONALD | WALLACE |
| DOHERTY | | | WRIGHT |

Part I: Texas People

# Part II:
# Texas Regions

Texas Crosswords

# The Panhandle

The Texas Panhandle is dominated by ranches and farms. Cattle dot the landscape, along with cotton and sunflower fields. The area has the look of the Old West. The Panhandle abuts Oklahoma to the east and north and New Mexico to the west. The Canadian River bisects the otherwise arid region, as does Interstate 40.

The major municipalities include Amarillo, Lubbock, Wichita Falls and Abilene. Traditional western wear—leather boots, hats, big belt buckles and jeans—is common attire for the natives. Locally made leather goods are readily available.

Amarillo, with about 300,000 residents, is the largest city in the Panhandle. The famous historic Route 66 runs through the Amarillo, which is one of the windiest city in the U.S. Travelers also enjoy a few unique attractions—the Cadillac Ranch and the Big Texan Steak Ranch. The former is an art display (not an actual ranch) featuring many colorful painted Cadillacs that are half buried, head first, in the ground. Tourists spray paint their names and other messages on the cars. The Big Texan Steak Ranch is famous for its 72-oz. steak challenge – eat a meal of shrimp cocktail, baked potato, Salad, roll with butter and a 72-oz. steak in one hour and it's free (if not, you owe $72!).

Lubbock is home to Texas Tech University and its Red Raiders. This area is also known as a huge cotton-growing region. Only the most adventurous visitors head to the small town of Sweetwater in March. The World's Largest Rattlesnake Roundup is held each year. This festival of sorts features the hunt as well as the crowing of Miss Snake Charmer, a rattlesnake parade and more.

The Panhandle offers lots of tamer outdoor activities. Lake Meredith and the Palo Duro Canyon State Park are popular recreational areas. Known as the "Grand Canyon of Texas," Palo Duro Canyon is 120 miles long, 20 miles wide and 800 feet deep. State Park visitors enjoy hiking, horseback riding, mountain biking and camping. Lake Meredith is a reservoir that was historically a source of drinking water for Amarillo and Lubbock. The lake was formed by Sanford Dam on the Canadian River. The lake opened in the early 2000s as a National Recreation Area. Visitors enjoy fishing, swimming, tubing, boating and camping. The lake is full of prized fish, including walleye and sand bass.

Buffalo Lake National Wildlife Refuge, with prairies, marshes and canyons to explore, is another intriguing area in the Panhandle.

The Big Texan in Amarillo is located on the famous "Mother Road" Route 66. Famous for its quality steaks and 72-oz steak challenge, the Big Texas is more than a restaurant. It is also a brewery, hotel, and RV park.

Texas Crosswords

# Panhandle Crossword
Solution on page 144.

## Across
1. East Moon cuisine
5. Muleshoe Police "bracelets"
10. Buckos
14. Torchy's slogan: "___ Good Tacos"
15. ___ Lama
16. Rapper whose name sounds like a drink
17. Love letter abbr.
18. Battle of San Jacinto weapon
19. Purplish shade
20. McAlister's Deli loaf

## Down
1. Red Raiders QB stats
2. Hem and ___
3. "The Yellow Rose of Texas"
4. Like the Borger News-Herald printing press
5. Citizens Bank offerings
6. Local 848 union
7. Lash
8. Jill's portrayer on Charlie's Angels
9. Bottom of a Buddy Holly platter
10. Back talk

## Part II: Texas Regions

### Across (cont.)

22. Sprouted
24. Outlaws & Legends country music festival mo.
25. Half a cocktail at Robbins Nest
27. ___-Caps (theater candy)
30. Home of Hardin-Simmons University
32. Dallas Texans org.
33. Successor to Holder as attorney general
35. Slowly, to the New Texas Symphony Orchestra
36. Restaurant reviews site
38. ___ culpa
39. Mean Woman Grill sandwich inits.
40. Not reporting for duty to the Texas National Guard
41. Top 'O Texas Rodeo site
43. "We're in trouble!"
47. Big thumbs-down
49. Downtown Farmers Market corn purchase
50. Grape soda brand
51. Texas landmark to remember
54. Word of regret
56. LBJ's successor
57. "Hub City"
59. Suffix with auction
60. Ballpark fig.
61. Golf great Ernie
62. World of Beer head
64. Magnolia Beach bottle letters
66. Drain stopper
68. Main St. one-eighty
71. They have their pluses and minuses
74. Machu Picchu locale
75. Like some of the clothes at Vintage Rose
76. While lead-in
77. Sam Houston Race Park chances
78. The Big Bang Salon lock of hair
79. 6/6/44

### Down (cont.)

11. Insight
12. Uncork'd Wine Bar transfer
13. Half of quadraphonic
21. Subj. for immigrants
23. Former Texas Supreme Court Justice Wilson
25. Poet Angelou
26. Not many
28. Lorelei, for one
29. Draft category
31. Reveal
34. Duncan & Boyd Jewelers carved piece
37. Carpenter's gadget
39. Lonestar Ballet support
42. Whittle down
44. "Beef Capital of the World"
45. Xcel Energy units
46. "This answer ends with a T," e.g.
48. Blunder
51. Embattled Syrian city
52. Put off guard
53. Nonsensical
54. Dallas Stars player, e.g.
55. Jr. and Sr. at Texas Tech
58. Carson County judge's workplace
63. Remote control button
65. ___ Piper
67. Rooster Teeth Podcast host Sorola
69. Texas City Terminal and Texas Pacifico (Abbr.)
70. Thumbs-down responses
72. Fort Meade org.
73. 4-H hog pen

## Munday Sudoku

Use logic to fill in the grid so every row, column and 2x3 box contains the letters M–U–N–D–A–Y, in honor of the Knox County town. It is home to the Munday High School Moguls. Solution on page 144.

|   |   | A | Y |   | U |
|---|---|---|---|---|---|
|   |   |   |   | A |   |
|   | U |   |   |   | D |
| N |   |   |   | M |   |
|   | M |   |   |   |   |
| D |   | Y | M |   |   |

## Southland Sudoku

Use logic to fill in the boxes so every row, column and 3x3 box contains the letters S–O–U–T–H–L–A–N–D, in honor of the Garza County community that lies along the eastern edge of the Llano Estacado. Solution on page 144.

| O |   | N |   |   |   |   | S | A |
|---|---|---|---|---|---|---|---|---|
|   | U | S | L |   |   |   | H |   |
|   |   |   |   | S |   |   |   | O |
|   |   |   | U |   | S |   | O |   |
|   |   |   | L |   | II |   | D |   |
|   | S |   |   | N |   | T |   |   |
| S |   |   |   | T |   |   |   |   |
|   | H |   |   |   |   | D | O | N |
| D | O |   |   |   |   |   | S | L |

Part II: Texas Regions

# One and Only One Vega

Find the one and only complete Vega in the grid, in honor of the county seat of Oldham County. Solution on page 144.

| V | G | E | A | E | V | V | G | A | E | V | E | G | E | V |
|---|---|---|---|---|---|---|---|---|---|---|---|---|---|---|
| E | G | A | V | G | E | A | V | E | G | G | E | V | A | E |
| G | A | E | V | E | A | G | E | E | G | V | E | G | V | G |
| V | E | G | G | A | E | V | G | G | A | V | A | G | V | E |
| V | E | G | G | V | V | E | G | E | V | G | E | V | G | A |
| E | G | A | V | E | G | E | G | A | V | E | G | G | A | E |
| V | G | E | A | A | A | G | G | G | E | E | E | V | V | V |
| E | V | G | A | V | G | G | E | E | V | E | E | G | E | E |
| G | E | E | G | V | A | V | G | E | A | G | V | A | G | V |
| E | V | G | A | G | E | G | A | A | A | G | E | A | E | A |
| V | A | G | A | G | G | E | A | A | V | G | E | E | G | V |
| E | A | G | G | A | V | V | A | E | E | G | A | G | E | G |
| G | V | E | V | V | A | V | V | A | V | E | V | E | A | E |
| V | A | G | E | E | V | G | A | E | V | V | G | A | V | E |
| E | V | E | A | E | G | A | E | G | A | E | V | G | E | V |

## North Central Texas

North Central Texas, otherwise known as the Metroplex, is influenced by the cities of Dallas, Fort Worth and the surrounding suburbs. With a metropolitan population of just under 5 million, the Dallas-Fort Worth region is the ninth-most populous area in the nation, and it is the most populous area in the state.

Among the attractions of "The Big D" are Deep Ellum (neighborhood and brewing company), World Aquarium, Telephone Pioneer Museum of Texas, Museum of Natural History and a number of John F. Kennedy memorials and museums.

Texans in this part of the state are avid football fans. In fact, the country's most expensive high school football stadium is in Allen, a suburb just north of Dallas. Eagle Stadium cost $60 million and holds 18,000 fans.

In nearby Fort Worth, "Where the West Begins", you can find the Sid Richardson Museum (a superb collection of western art), the National Cowgirl Museum and Hall of Fame, the Will Rogers Memorial Center, Kimbell Art Museum, Sundance Square and the Fort Worth Stockyards National Historic District. This 98-acre area is a former livestock market that opened in 1866 and thrived until the 1950s. Today the Stockyards contains entertainment and shopping venues, though many of the original structures remain. M.L. Leddy's, a famous cowboy boot and western wear company, is located in the Stockyards. Many Texans splurge at Leddy's, buying custom-made boots that will last a lifetime.

Despite the modern urban feel to North Central Texas, residents are just a short drive away from outdoor recreational activities. Richard Chambers Reservoir, Cedar Creek Reservoir, Lake Tawakoni, Lavon Lake, Grapevine Lake, Lake Lewisville and Ray Roberts Lake provide locals and tourists boating, fishing, hunting and hiking opportunities among the confluence of major highways.

The area is home to the Mesquite ProRodeo Series, held April to September. This is the country's best-known rodeo and has launched the careers of numerous riders and ropers. The competition includes professional bronc and bull riding, barrel racing, steer wrestling and more. Visitors can even have their pictures taken on a bull and ride ponies.

One of Texas's most famous ranches is Southfork, made famous as the setting of the popular TV show Dallas. The ranch in Parker now offers conference and event facilities as well as tours, trail rides and more.

Other major cities (and suburbs) include Arlington, Irving, Plano, and Garland.

Established in 1975 in Fort Worth, Texas, the National Cowgirl Museum and Hall of Fame is dedicated to honoring women of the American west who have displayed estraordingary courage and pioneering fortitude.

# Texas Crosswords

## Dallas Crossword

Solution on page 144.

### Across
1. Houston rocket org.
5. Sotomayor colleague
10. Slang for heroin
14. Texas Senate coalition
15. Uncle Calvin's Coffeehouse draw
16. Not fancy at all
17. Dallas State Correctional Institution confines
18. More epic

### Down
1. KXAS net.
2. Blackfriar Pub pint
3. Sunroom
4. Free speech org.
5. Hawaiian healer
6. Caribbean resort isle
7. Type of disco dancer
8. The Potter's House hymn ender
9. FWPD drug buster

Part II: Texas Regions

## Across (cont.)

19. Tom Landry: An Autobiography cover ID
20. Trinity River nature facility
23. HST predecessor
25. Santa ___ winds
26. Part of a Willie Nelson song
27. Teahouse hostess
29. Mughlai Indian Cuisine wrap
32. Some Mavs endings
33. Use a DPD taser on
34. Sense of taste
36. Where to see a Degas in Dallas
40. Dallas County candidate list
41. "Holy moly!"
44. Mokara Salon, e.g.
47. "Damn Yankees" seductress
48. Mooch
50. Houston Chronicle columnist Grieder
52. Poet for whom the Edgar Awards are named
53. Many millennia to the State Geological Survey
54. Dallas home to sea animals
59. "SOS" group
60. Dallas Fencers Club movement
61. Tex. House members
64. Devil's Bowl Speedway transmission choice
65. Tiny parasites
66. Tiny annoyance
67. Advantage
68. Part of SUV
69. Site for handicrafts

## Down (cont.)

10. "Rise and ___!"
11. Ex-Cuban president
12. Ideally
13. Lucky Dog Books varieties
21. Morse word
22. Mrs. Peron
23. Cowboys kickers stats
24. Tigers, on Globe Life Park scoreboards
28. Social slight
29. Pago Pago's place
30. Oodles
31. UK fliers
34. Word on a Moody Performance Hall door
35. Therefore
37. Green House Market menu option
38. "Do Ya" rock grp.
39. Urban dwelling
42. ___ trip
43. Buddhist branch
44. Dallas Water Utilities waste
45. Dug into
46. Cowboy Toyota safety device
48. Most achy
49. Fountain Place architect
51. Diplomat ___ Boothe Luce
52. Kindred Hospital on-call doctor's gadget
55. Aid to Dallas' poor
56. Witty bit
57. Golden rule preposition
58. Press for
62. ___ de deux
63. Texas Pork Producers home

73

Texas Crosswords

# East Texas

East Texas is commonly referred to as Piney Woods. There are four national forests in East Texas—Sabine, Angelina, Davy Crockett and San Jacinto—that combine for more than 11 million acres of woodland. At Angelina National Forest, visitors enjoy hiking and bird watching. The forest is home to the red-cockaded woodpecker, an endangered species. It is also a winter habitat for bald eagles. An interesting attraction is the Aldridge Sawmill Historic Site, which dates back to 1905 and has four remaining buildings.

The region is not without urban areas, as it is home to Houston, a metropolitan area with a population of 4.4 million. Houston's attractions include Hermann Park, the Museum District, the Menil Collection, Rothko Chapel and NASA's Johnson Space Center. Downtown dwellers love The Galleria, a 375-store shopping complex that includes an ice skating rink, two high-rise hotels and three office towers. Houston also has the world's largest concentration of health care and research organizations, at the Texas Medical Center. Patients from across the country travel to Houston for expert treatment.

Houston continues to recover from Hurricane Harvey. In late August 2017, this storm caused severe flooding (of more than 50 inches) in the Houston area. The damage has been estimated to be up to $125 billion, making it one of the worst natural disaster in U.S. history.

East Texas is the birthplace of modern Texas. Stephen F. Austin began his colonization of the area among the Caddo Indians, who settled near Nacogdoches more than 10,000 years ago. For this reason, Nacogdoches is considered the oldest town in Texas. Nacogdoches is home to Stephen F. Austin State University and its amazing Mast Arboretum. The arboretum and botanical gardens, opened in 1985, consists of 10 acres of plants and flowers. Texas largest azalea garden

Part II: Texas Regions

is here. The Ruby Mize Azalea Garden contains 7,000 azaleas, along with camellias, hydrangeas and varies trees and shrubs.

Other cities in the area are Tyler, Longview and Huntsville. Tyler, called the "Rose Capital of America," is home to many rose farmers and producers. Though production has declined in recent years, by the late 1950s, more than 20 million plants were produced each year in here. Tyler is home to the country's largest rose garden. The Tyler Rose Garden has more than 38,000 rose bushes of 500+ varieties. The Tyler Rose Museum is a popular attraction, and the city hosts the annual Texas Rose Festival each October.

Originally named the Manned Spacecraft Center, the Lyndon B. Johnson Space Center is NASA's center for human spaceflight and houses training, research, and flight control facilities. The 100-building complex was nicknamed Space City in 1967 as NASA worked on putting a man on the moon.

# Texas Crosswords

## East Texas Crossword

Solution on page 145.

### Across
1. Grand entrance
7. Central Bank fixture
11. Astros stat
14. World's second smallest country
15. Slushy drink brand
16. OU, to UT
17. Houston's gateway to NASA
19. In shape
20. "Call me ___"
21. Tick off

### Down
1. Evenings, briefly
2. Alley ___
3. Genetic stuff
4. Implied
5. Nails a Lone Star College test
6. Scottish map word
7. Exodus peak
8. Had a part with The Ensemble Theatre
9. Trial balloon

## Across (cont.)

22. Raccoon kin
25. Texas Senate staffer
26. Rice final, for one
27. Little trickster
28. "Eww, no more!"
30. TiVo button
32. HPD buster
34. Botanical balm
37. Part of a Flintstone's yell
41. Where to visit Kidtropolis in Houston
44. More robust
45. Lavish affection
46. Olympian Lipinski
47. Big ___ soda
49. Peculiar
51. Some UH students
52. ZZ Top work
55. Persia, now
58. Joe Myers Ford/Lincoln inventory
60. Alley Theatre performance
61. Soaps, e.g.
63. "Beats me," in texts
64. Place in Houston with 400+ stores
68. Heron Lakes Golf Course support
69. Star Trek role
70. Some nobility
71. Conroe HS lineman
72. Co-Cathedral of the Sacred Heart area
73. Accountant's list

## Down (cont.)

10. "Always," in sonnets
11. Attach
12. "Ta-da!"
13. "___ while they're hot!"
18. Sent by PC
21. Change things up at the AD Players Theater
22. No-brainer
23. Nebraska city
24. Art Car Parade month
29. Deface
31. Houston Baptist U. URL ending
33. Bethel Church service providers
35. Lennon's lady
36. Latvia neighbor
38. Houston Zoo critter
39. Small donkey
40. Accumulate
42. Dr. of rap
43. BCM study, briefly
48. Serve a meal at Hugo's
50. Home of the Stars
52. Maliciousness
53. Ancient
54. Like Show Palace dancers
56. Staggers
57. Squabble
59. Operators
62. Jessica of Sin City
64. IAH wanding org.
65. ___ v. Wade
66. Texans passing stat
67. Balaam's mount

# Texas Crosswords

## Fairmount Sudoku

Use logic to fill in the boxes so every row, column and 3x3 box contains the letters F–A–I–R–M–O–U–N–T, in honor of the community located in the Sabine National Forest. Solution on page 145.

|   | R |   | T |   |   | I |   |   |
|   | U |   |   | F |   |   |   |   |
| I | O | T | R |   |   | A | N |   |
| T | I |   | O | R | U |   | A |   |
|   |   |   | T |   | I |   |   |   |
|   | F |   | A | M | N |   | U | I |
|   | M | A |   |   | T | I | F | R |
|   |   |   | M |   |   |   | O |   |
|   | N |   |   | I |   |   | T |   |

## Shifted Fairmount Sudoku

Now try this. The same letters (F–A–I–R–M–O–U–N–T) in every row and column and 9-letter boxes, but the boxes have been shifted. Try it. Solution on page 145.

|   |   |   |   | M | O |   |   |   |
|   |   |   |   | T |   | F |   | O |
| U | N |   |   |   |   |   | A |   |
|   |   | F | I |   |   | N |   |   |
|   |   |   | N |   |   | U |   | I |
|   |   |   | A |   | T |   |   |   |
|   | R | N |   |   |   |   |   |   |
| T |   |   |   |   |   |   |   | U |
|   |   | A |   | F |   |   | M |   |

78

Part II: Texas Regions

## People from Houston Word Search

Solution on page 145.

```
T Y O F N A Q E F C D S Y Z R
M T T O C S D Q E F A P H D F
B A D V F K T M G M P A B I O
E X N F V D R Z O N L E M A R
Y M U D N P A H P L L E D U E
O D K C R R T N E H S U B Q M
N C M R O E E N D R G T C W A
C L W V G K L T U E E N U D N
E E R J E A S L I X R T U N C
K M H B R B K L F K K S T O E
B E Z O S S M I T H N F O O Y
F N Y K C A L B V D R O F N N
S S Q S T S E L W O N K R T U
G S B E K A D L U G S V N C Y
G H A J P Q T U L M S L D S A
```

| | | |
|---|---|---|
| ALLEN | CRONKITE | QUAID |
| ANDERSON | DELL | RETTON |
| BAKER | DUFF | ROGERS |
| BEYONCE | FORD | SCOTT |
| BEZOS | FOREMAN | SMITH |
| BLACK | FOYT | THOMAS |
| BUSH | KNOWLES | TUNE |
| CLEMENS | MANDRELL | YOUNG |

Texas Crosswords

# City Grid

The names of these East Texas cities are listed in alphabetical order according to length. Fit them into their proper places in the grid on the next page. We've started your solving by placing the city NEWTOWN (make certain you mark it off the list). Now look for a five-letter word that begins with a T. Continue working that way until you've filled in the grid. But be careful. There might be a city that seems to work in more than one place, but each city is used just once. Solution on page 145.

| 5 Letters | 6 Letters | 7 Letters | 8 Letters |
|---|---|---|---|
| AVERY | CENTER | ATLANTA | CARTHAGE |
| BURKE | CONROE | BAYTOWN | KINGWOOD |
| CASON | DAYTON | BRONSON | LONGVIEW |
| CHEEK | MINDEN | CLAYTON | MARSHALL |
| HOMER | NEWTON | KILGORE | PEARLAND |
| JAMES | ORANGE | LEGGETT | |
| PLUCK | PAXTON | NORWOOD | |
| SALEM | SUMNER | WEBSTER | |
| TATUM | WILLIS | ZAVALLA | |
| TYLER | WINNIE | | |

Part II: Texas Regions

# Texas Crosswords

## Texas Building Blocks

Read the clues and fill in the appropriate boxes, starting at the top. The answer to the second clue is the answer to the first clue, minus one letter. The answer to the third clue is the answer to the second clue, minus one letter, and so on. (The order of the letters may change.) Solution on page 145.

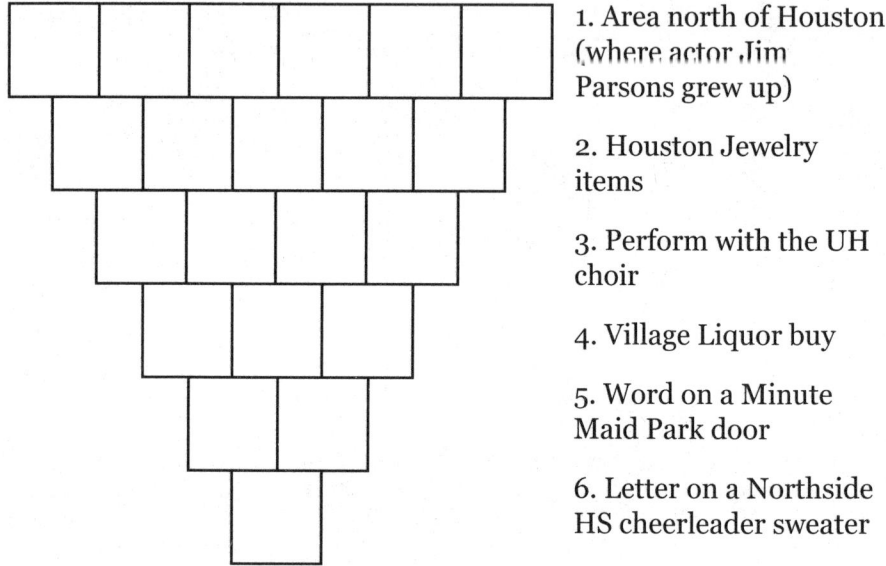

1. Area north of Houston (where actor Jim Parsons grew up)

2. Houston Jewelry items

3. Perform with the UH choir

4. Village Liquor buy

5. Word on a Minute Maid Park door

6. Letter on a Northside HS cheerleader sweater

Part II: Texas Regions

## Houston Astros All-Stars Word Search

Solution on page 145.

```
J G C K I J B R J C O R R E A
W A G N E R U H W U S R J J D
H K M N D J A N N Y W A Q O A
O I G G I B T G K N A C B L J
F N H S Y L S C R A L L R A E
G A P K B B G E S M T R F U T
Z R R M E N K E P G O A Y V Z
H T N R O R T S R E W R H A O
L L O Q E T G N I R A D T O N
L E D I O L X E N B T U O O I
E B D C H G L M G P S Y S Q N
W Q S G Q A R E E E O T W T L
G C E D E N O L R E N V V G Z
A L T U V E E C B E R K M A N
B S T U I K S N E V E D T W X
```

| | | |
|---|---|---|
| ALTUVE | CORREA | RYAN |
| BAGWELL | CRUZ | SCOTT |
| BELTRAN | DEVENSKI | SPRINGER |
| BERKMAN | DIERKER | STAUB |
| BIGGIO | FARRELL | TEJADA |
| BREGMAN | MENKE | WAGNER |
| CEDENO | MORTON | WATSON |
| CLEMENS | OSWALT | WYNN |

## South Texas

The Rio Grande River and Gulf of Mexico define South Texas. The Rio Grande cities of McAllen, Laredo, Eagle Pass and Del Rio border Mexico and give the region a little Mexico flavor and lifestyle. The area has some of the biggest and best vegetable farms in the nation. As there is little chance of frost, even home gardeners have success growing potatoes, tomatoes, eggplants and other veggies.

The Gulf Coast is referred to as the Texas Riviera and is a vacation destination for tourists and Texas natives. The major coastal cities are Port Arthur, Galveston and Corpus Christi. Port Arthur is a fishing mecca; Galveston was settled by pirate Jean Lafitte in 1817; and Corpus Christi is the final port of call for the USS Lexington and is home to the Texas State Aquarium.

There are six historic districts in Galveston. It is home to more than 60 structures on the National Register of Historic places, including homes from the Civil War through World War II. The Strand National Historic Landmark District has numerous Victorian era buildings that are now antique stores, boutiques, restaurants and galleries. Galveston is known as "Oleander City" due to the evergreen shrubs that thrive here. Perhaps Galveston's most famous native was Jack Johnson, the first black world heavyweight boxing champion. The "Galveston Giant" is a controversial figure in the city's history, but he has been honored with a life-sized bronze statue and a namesake park.

Brownsville is the southernmost city in Texas and a gateway to Matamoros, Mexico. Padre Island, just north of Brownsville, is a popular spot for college students on spring break. This barrier island is home to Padre Island National Seashore. The beaches here are home to the rare Kemp's Ridley sea turtles and four other turtle species. The northern part of the island is perfect for surfing and fishermen love Bob Hall Pier. The island offers activities galore, from birding and hiking to kiteboarding and golfing. Dolphin cruises are popular, and lucky visitors can watch newly hatched sea turtles get released into the wild (mid-June to August).

Not far from Corpus Christi is King Ranch. This ranch is one of the world's largest, with more than 900,000 acres. It was founded in 1853, eight years after Texas joined the Union. Edna Ferber's book Giant (and the movie starring James Dean) was based on King Ranch.

*Courtesy of Carol M. Highsmith via the Library of Congress*

The USS Lexington, nicknamed the Blue Ghost, was named to honor a previous aircraft carrier that had been lost in the Battle of the Coral Sea. Now the ship is docked in Corpus Christi, Texas and serves as a museum.

# Texas Crosswords

## South Texas Crossword

Solution on page 146.

### Across

1. Bone-dry
5. "Caps Lock" or "Print Screen"
10. Crystal Beach Park roller coaster cry
14. Laredo land map
15. Macy's shirt size
16. Texas ___ Country
17. Texas Classic links org.
18. Tortuga Coastal Cantina salsa ingredient

### Down

1. Organ in a UTMB anatomy class
2. Part of UTEP
3. In tatters
4. Del Mar College footnote notation
5. Alka-Seltzer sounds
6. Party fare
7. South Texas TV station
8. Rice psych class topics
9. Craving
10. Gives a Texas lickin'

86

# Part II: Texas Regions

## Across (cont.)

19. Wrinkly fruit
20. Maverick County seat and home to the Fort Duncan Museum
22. South Texas Speedway dashboard inits.
23. Chemical suffix
24. Nile biter
25. Peewee's Pet Adoption hound
28. Silently agree to
30. Malaquite Campground fire remnant
33. King HS support grp.
34. Lozano Golf Center target
36. Sprouts Farmers Market corn buy
37. Sulk
38. "Sparking City by the Sea"
42. Zero at the Al Kruse Tennis Center
43. Snap Fitness chest muscle, briefly
44. Jr. and Sr. at Ball HS
45. Brews Brothers brew
46. Disney subsidiary
48. Book of Texas maps
52. ___ tunnel syndrome
54. Crystal Corral Stables food bit
56. Singer DiFranco
57. Install, as tiles
58. Island city that is the site of the Moody Gardens Aquarium
61. HPD unit
63. Stocking material
64. Leprechaun's land
65. "If it ___ broke..."
66. DPD rap sheet listing
67. Bite like a beaver
68. Neat
69. Point of view
70. Like some offerings at Clear Creek Winery

## Down (cont.)

11. Guadalupe Peak, e.g.
12. Building add-on
13. Pierce's character on The Son
21. "Dig in!"
22. Houston Livestock Show and Rodeo mo.
25. Holly feature
26. Needle holder
27. Rat-a-___
29. 43,560 square feet
31. Pilgrimage site
32. Scrooge's cry
35. Nye Elementary School student
37. "Hey, over here!"
38. Pepsi or RC
39. Like much of the Narvaez expedition
40. Texas driver's license info
41. Angered
42. Clippers, on a Toyota Center scoreboard
46. Foot the bill
47. Deodorant type
49. Mexican-American lady
50. Polar jacket
51. Tough
53. Smashburger serving
55. Stave off
58. Miss
59. China setting
60. Kind of lily
61. Day for most UH football games
62. Nintendo console
63. CD predecessors

## Combes Sudoku

Use logic to fill in the grid so every row, column and 2x3 box contains the letters C–O–M–B–E–S, in honor of the Cameron County town. It is located at Exit 30 on I-69E. Solution on page 146.

|   |   |   |   |   |   |
|---|---|---|---|---|---|
| S |   | T |   |   |   |
|   | E |   | N |   | H |
|   | H |   | E |   |   |
|   |   | S |   | N |   |
| A |   | N |   | H |   |
|   |   |   | E |   | H |

## Edinburg Sudoku

Use logic to fill in the boxes so every row, column and 3x3 box contains the letters E–D–I–N–B–U–R–G, in honor of the county seat of Hidalgo County. It is home to the Rio Grande Bible Institute and UT-Rio Grande Valley. Solution on page 146.

|   | B |   |   | D |   |   |   |
|---|---|---|---|---|---|---|---|
| D | N |   | I | E | R |   |   |
|   | G | I | E |   | R | N |   |
|   | B | D | N |   |   | I |   |
|   | D |   |   | E | N | B |   |
|   | E | G |   | R | I | D |   |
|   | I | U | D |   | B |   | R |
|   |   | E |   |   | U |   |   |

# Part II: Texas Regions

## Twin Counties

The names of two South Texas counties have been combined on each line. The letters of each county name are in the correct order, but you need to break apart the names to come up with the two counties. Answers on page 146.

1. DIMLASMITLLE _____

2. STCAMEARRRON _____

3. WILLZAPACYATA _____

4. HIKENDALEDGOY _____

5. BROREOKFUGSIO _____

6. JACKCALSONHOUN _____

7. WEMAVBBERICK _____

8. LIVGOLEIADOAK _____

---

While the town of Rockport was hit hard by Hurricane Harvey in 2017, the nearby "Big Tree" remains. Known as the oldest tree in Texas, the Coastal Live Oak is estimated at 1,000 to 2,000 years old. The famous tree has survived 50 natural disasters, including hurricanes, floods, wildfires, and droughts. The tree is in Goose Island State Park. It is 44 feet tall and the trunk's circumference is 35 feet. What is particularly impressive is the oak's crown spread, which is nearly 90 feet.

Texas Crosswords

## Cities Word Search

Solution on page 146.

```
U P J A L J W A C O P L A N O
A S A N A N T O N I O D W H K
Z W N F O R T W O R T H Q H U
S K E X N E E L L I K E K O L
J I D G O L U B B O C K C M A
F V A A S B M C K I N N E Y R
R J S R A R L I N G T O N C E
I S A L L A D Q J M L S D L D
S I P A E Z W S C A T E P A O
C R V N K G P K W T G A G Q X
O V W D Y Z L N O T S U O H Q
W I A M A R I L L O U C Q R K
F N C O R P U S C H R I S T I
F G R A N D P R A I R I E M Z
S Z K D A U S T I N Z B C C J
```

| | | |
|---|---|---|
| AMARILLO | FRISCO | LUBBOCK |
| ARLINGTON | GARLAND | MCKINNEY |
| AUSTIN | GRAND PRAIRIE | PASADENA |
| CORPUS CHRISTI | HOUSTON | PLANO |
| DALLAS | IRVING | SAN ANTONIO |
| EL PASO | KILLEEN | WACO |
| FORT WORTH | LAREDO | |

## Falcon Wordsmith

Using the letters F–A–L–C–O–N (a Zapata County community), see how many words of three or more letters you can make. We found about 14 fairly common words (plus 10 more not so common ones that are acceptable in a game of SCRABBLE). Proper nouns, foreign words, and abbreviations don't count. If you can find 12 or more words in 15 minutes, you're an All-State Wordsmith! Solution on page 146.

1. _____
2. _____
3. _____
4. _____
5. _____
6. _____
7. _____
8. _____
9. _____
10. _____
11. _____
12. _____

Texas Crosswords

# Central Texas

This area of the Lone Star State, much of which is known as Texas Hill Country, is full of rolling hills, blue lakes and historic sites. The limestone hills are home to the state flower—bluebonnets—as well as many streams and much wildlife.

Central Texas is also home to large towns—Austin, San Antonio and Waco.

San Antonio is the seventh-most populous city in the US. It is most famous for being the site of the Alamo, originally founded as a mission in 1718 and overrun by a Mexican army in 1836. San Antonio boasts a famous River Walk, the La Villita historic district, the Mission Hike and Bike Trail, Sea World, Six Flags-Fiesta, and Tower of the Americas.

Austin is the state capital and site of the main campus of the University of Texas. It is one of the fastest-growing cities in the US. Located on the Colorado River, highlights include the Neill Cochran House, O. Henry Home and Museum, the Governor's Mansion and UT football games. A trip to Austin would not be complete without some BBQ and Tex-Mex. The Downtown area is home to the Capitol building as well as many live music venues on Sixth Street. South Congress is another popular area. It features shopping, restaurants, coffee shops and more. Lady Bird Lake is a popular destination for recreation. Hikers and runners enjoy the shore trail, while water lovers can be found kayaking, rowing and paddle boarding. Most motorized watercraft are banned from the lake, so it is a peaceful spot.

Waco is home to the Texas Rangers Hall of Fame and Baylor University. The city sits on the Brazos River and features a scenic seven-mile riverwalk. The trail passes under the Waco Suspension bridge and is very popular among walkers and runners. Waco is the birthplace of Dr. Pepper. It was first created at Morrison's Old Corner Drug Store in 1885. Pharmacist Charles Alderton spent his free time at the soda fountain and eventually found a mix he—and the rest of Texas—enjoyed. At the Dr. Pepper Museum & Free Enterprise Institute, visitors can have a drink at Frosty's Soda Shop and learn the history of cola in the US.

No visit to Central Texas would be complete without a drive through the Hill Country and its small towns of Llano, Elgin, Fredericksburg and Luckenbach.

Located in the Hemisfair district of San Antonio, the Tower of the Americas houses a restaurant 750 feet above the ground. It is the tallest observation tower in Texas and provides panoramic views of San Antonio.

# Texas Crosswords

## Central Texas Crossword

Solution on page 147.

### Across
1. King in a Steve Martin song
4. Stone of La La Land
8. NASA scrub
13. Cain raiser
14. Have to have
15. Moses Jewelry gems
17. San Antonio marine park
19. Fancy tie
20. Strip of wood
21. KSAT's American ___

### Down
1. Musk's electric car
2. Eyes of Texas parts
3. Suckling spots
4. Another Green World musician
5. Fine wool
6. Fuse
7. Extension
8. Longhorns punt path
9. Explodes
10. 2009 Peace Prize Nobelist

Part II: Texas Regions

## Across (cont.)

23. Starbucks aroma
24. Give out homework at Krueger Middle School
26. Juice for Zeus
28. Austin driving hazard
30. UT profs' aides
31. "This means ___!"
34. 41-Across carrier
37. Battery fluid
39. Walking stick
40. Glorify
41. San Antonio airport code
42. Electrical pioneer
43. Cathedral of San Fernando place to pray
44. Laredo's county
45. Signed a contract with the Spurs
46. "Enough already!"
47. Tic-tac-toe win
48. Vast
50. Put in Travis State Jail
53. ___ wait (lurks)
57. Bisect
59. Astros pitcher's stat
61. Lopez de Santa ___
62. Cantilevered windows
64. Fiesta Texas amusement park operator
66. SAPD unit
67. 60 minutes
68. Understood
69. Eccentric
70. The Sun ___ Rises
71. Pigpen

## Down (cont.)

11. San Antonio pedestrian park
12. Blue hue
16. Cardinal letters
18. Frank Erwin Center ref's need
22. Beatles hit
25. Test for some TTU srs.
27. Scoundrel
29. Not liquid or solid
32. ACES Poker Room buy-in
33. Use the San Antonio Public Library
34. Job for Vallejo's Body Shop
35. St. Anthony Catholic HS midterm
36. San Antonio historic arts village
38. Austin city transport
39. Hide
42. Caesar's eight
44. Sichuan House pan
47. Leopardlike cat
49. Solar ___
51. For all to see
52. Turkish bigwig
54. Hose woes
55. Fort Knox bar
56. Ill-tempered
57. Skip preceder
58. Show horse
60. Six-stringed instrument
63. Like a fox
65. To and ___

Texas Crosswords

## Missing T–R–O–Y

Place the letters T–R–O–Y (for the Bell County city), once each, in any order to complete these common six-letter words. Answers on page 147.

1. F __ __ S __ __
2. N __ __ A __ __
3. __ U __ C __ __
4. __ H E __ __ __
5. __ __ G U __ __
6. __ __ __ P H __
7. __ __ S __ E __
8. P __ E __ __ __
9. S P __ __ __ __
10. S __ __ __ M __

Bonus: There is only one seven-letter word in the English language that ends with the letters T-R-O-Y (in that order). What is it? Hint: We'd give you a hint, but it would ruin you.

Part II: Texas Regions

# Famous Austinites Word Search
Solution on page 147.

```
I O J N P W M S R G K R L W N
D B B D G Y J I O O N L K W C
T R O G A N C J K N I K C I C
T N O S N H O J N Z L C I L O
E V O R A O D H X A P O D S S
C U A R N N R T H L O L D O E
W V D U U H W T Z E J L O N E
A S T Q G H E O S S V U R D R
F K O U K H P N R M X B E X B
R A T H E R A B R B R L G W Z
W A L L A C H N K Y L A A A W
C H J L E I S I K F E O Q I O
U Z S E T I H W R O H A W K E
N E L L Y F N A D R O J W Y Q
R E K L A W J L D D E I X A Q
```

| | | |
|---|---|---|
| ARMSTRONG | HAWKE | RODDICK |
| BREES | HENRY | ROGAN |
| BROWN | JOHNSON | ROVE |
| BULLOCK | JOPLIN | VAUGHAN |
| DELL | JORDAN | WALKER |
| FAWCETT | NELLY | WALLACH |
| FORD | RATHER | WHITE |
| GONZALES | RICHARDS | WILSON |

Texas Crosswords

# Find the Words

Starting anywhere in the box, use adjacent letters—vertically, horizontally or diagonally—to make as many words as you can from the letters in COTTONWOOD SHORES (a Burnet County city). Words need to be five or more letters and cannot use the same letter square more than once per word. No proper nouns, hyphenated or foreign words and no slang. We found about 40 fairly common words, but there are 62 words that can be made that are in The Official SCRABBLE Players Dictionary. Find 30 words in 30 minutes to earn induction into the Texas Solving Hall of Fame. List of words on page 147.

1. _____
2. _____
3. _____
4. _____
5. _____
6. _____
7. _____
8. _____
9. _____
10. _____
11. _____
12. _____
13. _____
14. _____
15. _____

16. _____
17. _____
18. _____
19. _____
20. _____
21. _____
22. _____
23. _____
24. _____
25. _____
26. _____
27. _____
28. _____
29. _____
30. _____

Part II: Texas Regions

## San Antonio Word Search

Solution on page 148.

```
U P B E C K E R W B W H I T E
U F T H H A M F R O L Y A T N
Y E C I S N E R O S M A X N O
C O C K R E L L T Z M K C D T
L K N I R E N B E R G I B K N
K L I C D A P Y S O B R T O R
S A E N M Z Y P C Y O Q S H O
X S E B G R T V W W C B T E H
J O L P V A O J N O A G E Z T
E O C F N G B Z L L S A V C A
S U N S K C I H E F T T E P N
N F I E F S N E S F R T S I E
O H D L S E M T T Q O I U W G
Y N Z M G H P H E Q G Q D F U
L B K S D S A Z R S M J T S X
```

| BECKER | GATTI | QUIN |
| BELL | HICKS | SMITH |
| BLACK | JONES | STEVES |
| BROWN | KING | TAYLOR |
| CASTRO | LESTER | THORNTON |
| CISNEROS | LYONS | TOBIN |
| COCKRELL | NIRENBERG | WHITE |
| GARZA | PEAK | WOLFF |

# Texas Crosswords

## West Texas

West Texas is closest to the stereotypical Texas of western movies and novels. Open spaces, big ranches, deserts, mountains, cowboys, and Indians are all in abundance.

For outdoors types, West Texas is a bonanza. Picturesque spots can be found at Davis Mountains Indian Lodge State Park, Big Bend National Park, and the Guadalupe Mountains National Park, site of the highest point in Texas (the Guadalupe Peak at 8,749 feet).

West Texas is less densely populated than the rest of Texas. It was once mostly home to Native American tribes, including the Apache, Comanche, and Kiowa. The area is generally dry and full of canyons, so there is not a lot of agriculture here. Major industries include petroleum and natural gas production, livestock, grain, and cotton. The countryside is dotted with wind farms and pumpjacks drilling for oil.

Major cities in the region are El Paso, San Angelo, Midland, Odessa, Ft. Stockton, and Alpine.

El Paso has a population of more than 500,000 and is across the Rio Grande from Ciudad Juarez, Mexico. El Paso is the site of Fort Bliss (a major military outpost), Chamizal National Memorial, the El Paso Mission Trail, and the Tigua Indian Reserve. The University of Texas at El Paso, founded in 1914, UTEP has serves a huge Mexican American student group. The campus is unique in that its buildings are in the Dzong (fortress) architectural style, modeled after those in Bhutan. The UTEP Miners play in Sun Bowl Stadium, which hosts the Sun Bowl each year.

Midland is an oil town with the Permian Basin Petroleum Museum and the Museum of the Southwest; just west of Odessa is a meteor crater formed more than 20,000 years ago; and Alpine's major attraction is the Museum of the Big Bend on the campus of Sul Ross State University.

Part II: Texas Regions

The David Crockett Monument, a 13-foot-tall granite memorial, is in Ozona. Known as "The Biggest Little Town in the World," it has a population of just 3,225. The town is located in Crockett County and hosts an annual festival in the Alamo hero's memory each August/September. This area is a huge producer of wool and mohair. It is also home to numerous wild javelina, piglike creatures that roam the deserts.

The Civilian Conservation Corps (CCC) built Davis Mountains State Park in 1933. The park was expanded aby Texas in 1967 and now coveres more than 2,700 acres.

101

# Texas Crosswords

## West Texas Crossword
Solution on page 148.

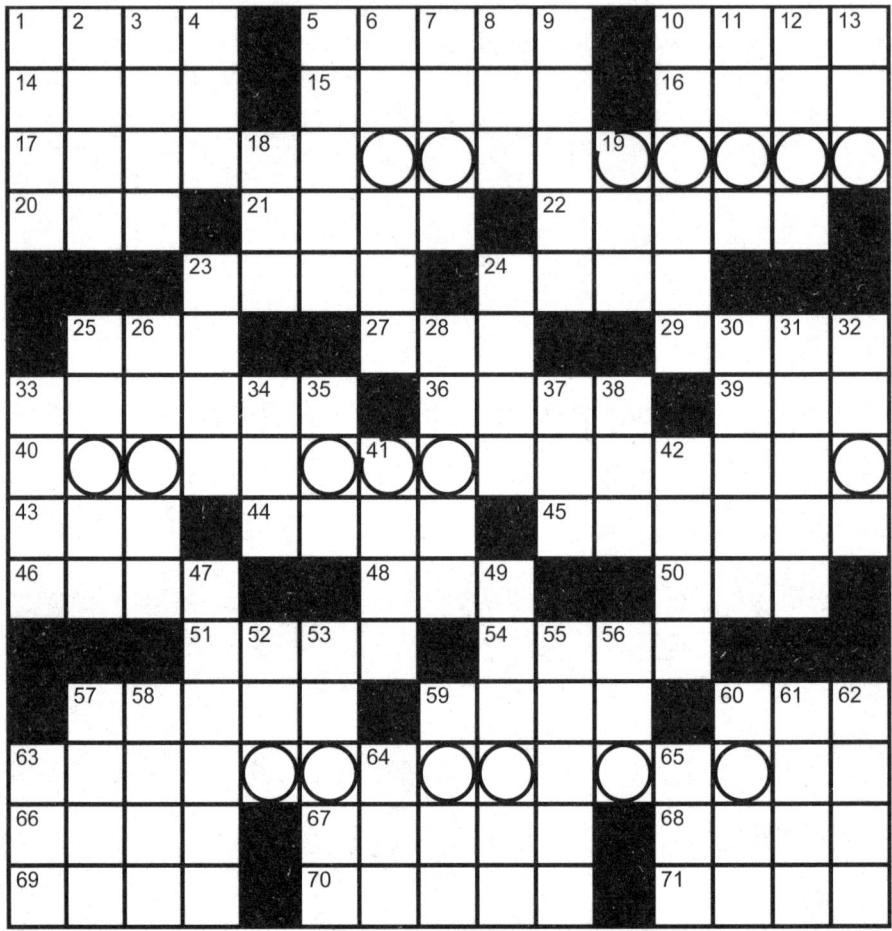

### Across
1. Tear go-with
5. Barely beat the Mavs
10. Challenge
14. Post-Anthony Flying Horse Half Marathon feeling
15. Dallas star Hagman
16. Flamboyance
17. Longed-for place, like the hometown of Laura Bush?
20. Silent film star Mix

### Down
1. Texstar Power unit
2. Caverns of Sonora effect
3. Throat-clearing sound
4. Tex. House member
5. Run off to wed
6. Kind of control
7. Crossword diagram
8. Yoakum County Hospital areas, briefly
9. Gigi's Hair Salon workers

Part II: Texas Regions

## Across (cont.)
21. Apple tablet
22. Coronado Prime Meats buy
23. Picture file format
24. Anthem opener
25. ELP govt. overseer
27. Del Rio lodge member
29. Soaks (up)
33. Dad
36. Ascarate Golf Course club
39. Vietnamese neighbor
40. Patriotic song about where Roy Orbison lived?
43. Beluga yield
44. Imitate a hot dog
45. Read through
46. Messes up
48. Texas School for the Deaf syst.
50. Sen. Cruz
51. Door fixture
54. Grander than grand
57. West Texas musical offering
59. "Good grief!"
60. UTEP dorm supervisors
63. Middle Eastern document for travel to Debbie Reynolds' birthplace?
66. The Hoppy Monk bar measure
67. Put up
68. Nike competitor
69. "Monster ___"
70. "Later!"
71. Close, like New Mexico

## Down (cont.)
10. MAF flight holdups
11. "Ah, me!"
12. Deliver a tirade
13. Coleman HS football lineman
18. Sunset Memorial Gardens tombstone letters
19. ___ good deed
23. Frame part
24. Gumbo ingredient
25. Chase Tower elevator stop
26. Calculator, at times
28. Rolls
30. Bottoms Up Bar garnish
31. Went back and forth
32. Fly high
33. Fairy tale villain
34. Matterhorn, e.g.
35. Class-conscious org.
37. Texter's "Wow!"
38. Opposite of paleo-
41. Ginger cookie
42. Texas A&M military grp.
47. Place for a sword
49. Inheritance
52. "___ we there yet?"
53. Fred Loya Insurance department
55. Cafe Italia staple
56. Texas driver's lic. and others
57. Dept. of Labor arm
58. Cowboys and Astros
59. Duel tool
60. Wander around Texas
61. 57-Across highlight
62. Fort Worth ___-Telegram
63. School of thought
64. Eur. land
65. Texas Soul Cafe kitchen item

Texas Crosswords

# Square Cities

Each square contains the 8-letter name of a city in the West Texas region. The name can be found by beginning at one of the letters and reading either clockwise or counterclockwise. Solution on page 148.

1.
| I | O | N |
|---|---|---|
| T |   | J |
| C | N | U |

4.
| A | R | A |
|---|---|---|
| S |   | G |
| A | S | O |

2.
| P | O | I |
|---|---|---|
| R |   | D |
| E | S | I |

5.
| T | H | O |
|---|---|---|
| A |   | N |
| R | A | M |

3.
| L | I | N |
|---|---|---|
| L |   | R |
| O | T | O |

6.
| D | S | H |
|---|---|---|
| O |   | E |
| O | W | R |

Part II: Texas Regions

## Colleges Word Search

Solution on page 148.

```
Y L U A U J N O R T H W O O D
T S O U T H W E S T E R N X Q
R O L Y A B I Q X B L T K M L
Z L T P A U L Q U I N N R & Z
N M N E R Y E K E A D I A B G
H V C O X L Y R R U M C M & S
D A R O T A & I & S T D L L C
N N I E G R S P Z T R I L A H
& O S H D & E A K I I A A M R
Q Y W Y O K I B & N N R H A E
T S E K G U H V M M I B I R I
S U L R O S S S T A T E R C N
D O L V J P T T H C Y Z V X E
P & X G C O N C O R D I A & R
H O W A R D P A Y N E P A R K
```

| | | |
|---|---|---|
| AMBERTON | HOWARD PAYNE | SCHREINER |
| AUSTIN | LAMAR | SOUTHWESTERN |
| BAYLOR | MCMURRY | SUL ROSS STATE |
| CONCORDIA | NORTHWOOD | TEXAS A&M |
| CRISWELL | PARK | TRINITY |
| HALLMARK | PAUL QUINN | WILEY |
| HOUSTON | RICE | |

# Part III:
# Michigan Activities

# Texas Crosswords

## Amused in Texas

Texas is one of the US's largest tourist destinations, and it's easy to see why. With destinations like the Alamo, Palo Duro Canyon, NASA, and Texas Hill Country, there's an unlimited supply of fun.

Called "The Grand Canyon of Texas," Palo Duro Canyon is actually a system of canyons in the Texas Panhandle near Amarillo. It is 120 miles long, making it the second-largest canyon in the US. At its highest point, it is 1,000 ft. Visitors admire the colorful rock layers, steep walls, and amazing formations.

History lovers flock to the Alamo in San Antonio, and science enthusiasts love to visit Space Center Houston.

Visitors to the Lone Star State's capital can find out for themselves how to "Keep Austin Weird." One of the most unique Austin occurrences is the nightly (March to October) emergence of 1.5 million bats from under the Ann W. Richards Congress Avenue Bridge. Huge crowds gather downtown to watch them pour out about 20 minutes before sunset. This colony of Mexican free-tailed bats—the largest urban bat colony in the world—leave their roost each night for dinner, creating a spectacle than must be seen to be believed.

While in Austin, the Cathedral of Junk is another site to behold. This amazing multi-level building, made solely of other people's castoffs (60 tons of junk), sits in a southside backyard. Creator Vince Hanneman's began building the Cathedral in 1988 and enjoys telling amazed tourists all about his yard art.

The west Texas town of Marfa is a destination that is definitely off the beaten track. Originally known for the "Marfa Lights," the desert town has more recently become known for its arts. Minimalist artist Donald Judd moved to Marfa in 1971 and began installing his art in two airplane hangars and other buildings. He later acquired more and more buildings with hopes of displaying large collections of individual artists' work. Judd's Chinati Foundation hosts installations on an old army base, and visitors can see unusual creations all over town. Many contemporary artists now live in the area.

Nine miles outside Marfa on Highway 90 is a viewing platform where visitors sometimes see the "Marfa Lights" (or Marfa Ghost Lights). This mysterious phenomenon, first spotted in 1883, is described as dancing, flickering, or twinkling orbs in the sky. The sometimes colorful lights have never been fully explained, though theories (paranormal activity, plasma, campfires, extremely distant car lights) abound.

Texas Hill Country is notable for its rugged limestone or granite hills. It is home to Enchanted Rock, the second largest granite dome in the United States.

*Courtesy of Carol M. Highsmith via the Library of Congress*

Texas Crosswords

# Neighbors Crossword
Solution on page 149.

## Across
1. No-goodniks
5. For the time being
11. "____ luck?"
14. Area about the size of the Cowboys field
15. Southwest Eye Institute focal point
16. ____ Speedwagon
17. TTU sports org.
18. NRA president North

## Down
1. Defeatist's word
2. Give in
3. UNT art class student, at times
4. A-Plus Tailor line
5. Representative
6. Type of Rangers pitcher
7. Ear-related
8. Binge-watcher's device
9. Midland-to-Fort Worth dir.
10. Wetland area

110

## Part III: Michigan Activities

### Across (cont.)
19. Ex-Baylor president Starr
20. Texas neighbor
22. Serenity Massage Therapy, e.g.
24. Texas Poet Laureate tribute
25. Caustic chemical
26. Texas Lottery ticket
29. ___ cotta
31. Renown
34. Ivan the Terrible, e.g.
35. Middle number of El Paso's area code
37. Ravens, on AT&T Stadium scoreboards
38. Aladdin prince
39. Rare forecast for KPRC meteorologists
42. Texas pol concern
44. ___ of Capri Casino
45. John H. Kirby State Forest tree
46. Picked up
47. Prohibit
49. Legal rights org.
51. Listen to
53. "Who's there?" reply
57. McDonald Observatory heavenly body
59. Aged
61. FC Dallas goose egg
62. Popular fruit drink
63. Texas neighbor
66. GI entertainers
68. University of Texas of the Permian Basin locale
70. Reason to call Midway Plumbing
71. Abilene Garden Club flower, for short
72. Fridge raider
73. West Texas Eye cataract site
74. Soup Man veggie
75. Square dance groups
76. Barely beat the Texans

### Down (cont.)
11. Texas neighbor
12. Texas College alumna bio word
13. Hither's partner
21. Panache
23. Rapper Fat ___
26. Rockets' A-list invitee
27. Mint Poker action
28. Great Lakes city
30. Spurs ticket info
32. Decrease
33. Texas Highways, e.g.
36. JR Pockets black ball
39. KVUE daytime offering
40. Salt, in a Rice chem class
41. Texas neighbor
43. Country singer Bandy
44. Central Bank CD yield
48. Pitches in
50. Prefix with sex
52. Put out
54. Grabbed
55. Westmoreland Coal Co. work
56. Pass, as time
58. ___ Lodge
60. Newton County Court perjurers
63. For fear that
64. DOL watchdog
65. Sit in I-20 traffic
66. Minute Maid Park strike caller
67. Take to Freestone County Court
69. West Houston Medical Center MD

Texas Crosswords

## He Said What?

Fill in the blanks with the words provided to form a quote from Tommy Lee Jones. Solution on page 149.

"I STILL _____ _____ THE _____ THING I'M _____ _____ IS _____ A _____ FROM _____ ."

BEING          PROBABLY
BOY            SUITED
FOR            TEXAS
ONLY           THINK

---

In 2007, Hollywood hit Marfa. Two movies nominated for Academy Awards for Best Picture were filmed in the small town at the same time. The winner, *No Country for Old Men* starred Texan Tommy Lee Jones along with Javier Bardem and Josh Brolin. The thriller was written and directed by Joel and Ethan Coen and is set in West Texas in 1980. It tells the story of a Texas welder and Vietnam War veteran.

The other film, *There Will Be Blood*, starred Daniel Day-Lewis. It is the story of an oilman in search of wealth during California's oil boom. Marfa was the film's center of production, unlike *No Country*, which used Marfa for just certain scenes.

Some conflicts arose between the two sets. *No Country* had to pause filming for a day due to huge amounts of smoke coming from the *Blood* set.

Part III: Michigan Activities

## Texas Fauna

With its mild winters and variety of landscapes, Texas is home to many interesting animals. Three species are considered the official mammal—the nine-banded armadillo, the Texas longhorn and the Mexican free-tailed bat.

The longhorn is, of course, a breed of cattle known for its horns that can reach almost six feet across. It is also the University of Texas mascot—"Bevo" is one college football's most recognizable symbols. Bevo is burnt orange in color, but longhorns come in a range of hues; dark red and white mixes are the most common. Despite their tough appearance, they are intelligent and have gentle dispositions, so they are often trained as riding steers.

Of course longhorns are not Texas' most common animal. The state has more cattle than 43 states have people. About 13% of all U.S. cattle are from Texas, and the total value of the state's cattle and calves is more than $8.5 billion.

The armadillo is a hard-shelled animal the size of a small dog. They have powerful claws that they use to dig for food. They often eat grubs, which are harmful to many crops. It's no wonder Texans are quite proud of this critter and have adopted it as an unofficial mascot.

The Mexican free-tailed bat is a common but rarely seen animal. The creature lives throughout the southern half of the U.S. and roost mainly in caves. They also like buildings with dark recesses in ceilings or walls. There are numerous colonies in Texas. Bracken Cave, north of San Antonio, hosts the largest colony, at about 20 million bats. The most famous colony is probably in Austin, living under the Congress Avenue Bridge near downtown. People gather at dusk each night to watch the creatures emerge for dinner.

Texas wildlife is quite varied. Mammals include coyotes, wolves, bears, raccoons, bobcats, jaguars and mountain lions.

The Gulf of Mexico waters off Texas are home to many creatures, including whales, dolphins, sea turtles, manatees and seals.

# Texas Crosswords

Texas' marshes, swamps, rivers and lakes are also home to numerous wild things, including alligators. With at least 500,000 gators in the state, only Louisiana and Florida have more. The population had dwindled to just a few thousand in the late 1960s, but state and federal protection laws have helped them rebound. While alligators can be found across the state, they are most common in southeast Texas and along the coast.

Other common wildlife in Texas include snakes, lizards, birds and jackrabbits.

The state bird is the Northern Mockingbird. This beautiful bird has gray to brown upper feathers and a paler belly. The white patches on it tail and wings are mainly visible when they are in flight. It is the only species of mockingbird found in North America, and the bird is known for its intelligence.

The black-tailed jackrabbit is often found the Texas deserts. The rabbit grows to about three to six pounds and two feet in length. It is the third-largest hare found in North America. The characteristic that distinguishes the jackrabbit from a regular rabbit is its very long ears. It also has long powerful rear legs.

Texas is one of only 12 states to have an official state dog breed. The Lacy Dog (or Blue Lacy Dog) is a breed of working dogs that were discovered in Texas in the mid-1800s. The vast majority of these animals are still found in the Lone Star State.

The Lacy is strong and fast, making it perfect for hunting and herding. The dogs are very intelligent and quick to learn; they love to work with big game and livestock and are typically farm or ranch dogs. While this breed can be a great companion, having the Lacy as a family pet is challenging. The dog will need lots of activity, a job and room to roam.

These dogs come in three color varieties. The typical Texas blue ranges from light silver to dark charcoal. They may also be "red" (cream to rust) or tricolor (blue with red).

Courtesy of Carol M. Highsmith via the Library of Congress

This breed of cattle was bred for a high drought tolerance and are the descendants of the first cattle brought to the Americas by Christopher Columbus and other Spanish colonists.

## Texas State Symbols

Air Force: Commemorative Air Force
Bird: Northern mockingbird
Bread: Pan de campo
Cooking implement: Dutch oven
Dinosaur: Brachiosaur Sauropod
Dish: Chili
Dog: Blue Lacy
Domino Game: Texas 42
Fiber and fabric: Cotton
Fish: Guadalupe bass
Flower: Bluebonnets
Folk dance: Square dance
Fruit: Texas red grapefruit
Gem: Texas blue topaz
Grass: Sideoats grama
Insect: Monarch butterfly
Mammal (small): Nine-banded armadillo
Mammal (large): Texas Longhorn
Mammal (flying): Mexican free-tailed bat
Molecule: Buckyball
Music: Western swing
Musical instrument: Acoustic guitar
Nut: Native pecan
Pastries: Strudel and sopaipilla
Pepper: Chiltepin
Plant: Prickly pear cactus
Plays: "Fort Griffin Fandangle"
Reptile: Texas horned lizard
Shell: Lightning whelk
Ship: USS Texas
Shrub: Crape myrtle
Snack: Tortilla chips and salsa
Soil: Houston Black
Sport: Rodeo
Stone: Petrified palmwood
Tartan: Texas bluebonnet
Tree: Pecan
Vegetable: Texas sweet onion

Texas Crosswords

## Lone Star Crossword

Solution on page 149.

### Across
1. Riva's Italian Restaurant farewell
5. Mayhill Hospital test
9. Houston Symphony woodwind
13. Part of a foot
14. Christmas season
15. Country singer Keith
16. Miller Ad Agency rep
19. SHO alternative
20. Aliens, for short
21. "___ Abner"

### Down
1. KGB counterpart
2. Monsters, ___
3. Notre Dame's conf.
4. "Oops!"
5. St. John Lutheran Church council
6. Galleria Nails polish brand
7. Out of the wind on Lake Amistad
8. Drink of the gods
9. Giant Hall-of-Famer
10. Cast Iron Grill kitchen direction

116

## Part III: Michigan Activities

### Across (cont.)
22. KSAT net.
25. End of UT's URL
27. Inquire
29. Texas tea
31. "Wheel of Fortune" singer
33. Camera inits.
35. Musical work
37. Pueblo Indian
38. AUS overseer
39. Bluefire Photography finish
40. Not eligible for the NBA's annual player picks
43. Said "Paper or plastic" at H-E-B Grocery
46. Abilene Christian pysch class topic
47. "Cogito ___ sum"
51. Hometown of Olympic champ Carly Patterson
52. SAT screening org.
53. Fire remnant
54. LT Corner Pub order
55. Big bird at Willow Grove Ranch
57. AFC South, e.g.
59. "As I see it," online
60. Pas' mates
62. Assn.
64. Houston Dynamo goose egg
66. Microsoft browser
72. Close by, like Oklahoma
73. "___, Brute?"
74. Texas tie
75. Barely beat the Cowboys
76. Capital Medical Clinic directive
77. Crafty website

### Down (cont.)
11. Plain as day
12. Peeper protectors
17. United Cab alternative
18. Battleship letters
22. ___ Wednesday
23. "Takin' Care of Business" band, to fans
24. Minute Maid Park souvenir
26. Fort Sam Houston org.
28. Sushi Place wrap
30. "Law," on a bilingual workroom poster
32. Mountain crest
34. Certain Sherwin-Williams paints
36. Tribal emblem
38. Craze
39. "Frankenfood" letters
41. Actress Russo
42. "Good grief!"
43. State Fair of Texas barn sound
44. Hoarder's cry
45. Slowly picked up
48. Astros stat
49. Kubes Jewelers stone
50. Acapulco gold
52. Football Hall-of-Famer from Hardin-Simmons: Bulldog ___
53. Satanic
56. Rangers dugout VIP
58. Suggestions
61. Guys-only party
63. US Rep. Gallego
65. Ear part
67. "___ he drove out of sight…"
68. Baylor books
69. Go bad
70. 1997 US Open winner
71. Dale's singing cowboy

Texas Crosswords

## Texas U Alumni Word Search

Solution on page 149.

```
Q E O Z X S B M O C C M I B Z
R I T T E R R L N O S N H O J
S C K I T E I T L Q Q D I T O
C L A R K P P C J E L N C I P
E G O A Z T V N H E D H K L L
R B B J T Y R T I A B Z S L I
E J Y M G E L F T E R R Z E N
G K N R K H S L N O Y D U R R
E G D R D N B T A O B Z S S E
W I A K A N S U V N S B V O T
L P Z M N E A T S A N L A N T
L Y N Z N A X L Z H F O I M O
E G F A W C E T T V H A C W N
Z E I P P D E B D C O N R W T
H U T C H I S O N F T E U K J
```

|          |           |           |
|----------|-----------|-----------|
| ABBOTT   | FAWCETT   | MCCOMBS   |
| BAKER    | HICKS     | PARKER    |
| BEAN     | HUTCHISON | RETTON    |
| BENTSEN  | JOHNSON   | RICHARDS  |
| BUSH     | JOPLIN    | RITTER    |
| CLARK    | KITE      | TILLERSON |
| CONNALLY | LANDRY    | WILSON    |
| DELL     | MANSFIELD | ZELLWEGER |

Part III: Michigan Activities

# Texas Flora

With its numerous biomes, Texas is a home to a great variety of plants, flowers and trees. Varieties vary from region to region and depend on rainfall frequency, type of soil and temperature/frost likelihood.

Texas's state tree is the pecan. These trees have grown in the Lone Star state before humans arrived. In fact, they can live more than 1,000 years and grow to more than 100 feet tall. Native Americans relied on pecans for much of their diet. The nuts are extremely popular today, often being used in baked goods, trail mixes and, of course, Texas' delicious state pie, the pecan pie. Pecan wood is used to make furniture, baseball bats, flooring and carvings.

Other majestic Texas trees include the Live Oak, Cedar Elm, Texas Ash, Southern Red Oak and various Evergreens.

As any Texas traveler can attest, the bluebonnet is an impressive flower. The lupine pops up all along Texas's roadways in the spring and huge flower fields abound. The flowers can reach up to three feet tall. There are numerous varieties, but the most common are the blue ones with bits of white. There are also pink and white bluebonnets. Scientists at Texas A&M created the maroon bluebonnet (one of the school colors).

Wildflowers have always been popping up along Texas highways, but the State doesn't take its bluebonnets for granted. The State delays mowing in the spring, giving bluebonnets and other wildflowers an opportunity to grow. Each year, the State plants about 30,000 pounds of wildflower seeds. Texans are serious in their love of bluebonnets. There are numerous bluebonnet festivals and thousands of tourists hit the road each spring in search of the beautiful fields.

Texas's agriculture industry is so strong that it even has an official state fruit—the Texas red grapefruit. This citrus is gown mainly in the Rio Grande Valley and is harvest in late winter to early spring. Apples, blackberries, blueberries, grapes, figs, and strawberries are other common crops.

# Texas Crosswords

## State Parks Crossword
Solution on page 149.

### Across
1. Sneaker, e.g.
5. Heathen
10. Nail Spa polish color
14. ___ Christian Andersen
15. Dodge the HPD
16. Mary Kay rival
17. The Dallas Morning News section
18. Hair Peace Salon 'dos
19. Video recorder

### Down
1. Texas Seafood Restaurant catch
2. Spy Mata ___
3. Like a KPRC newscast
4. To be, to Brutus
5. Coke competitor
6. Laredo st. crosser
7. State park on the Frio River in Hill Country
8. Navy bigwig
9. Angelina National Forest home

## Part III: Michigan Activities

### Across (cont.)

20. Frogmen
22. It may be picked
23. Get better
24. Downy duck
26. Neal Hamil Agency poser
27. Galveston Bible Church grace word
31. Neptune neighbor
33. Space cadet
35. Abner descriptor
36. Cul-de-___
39. State park near the Sam Rayburn Home
40. State park halfway between San Antonio and Austin
42. USN rank
43. Mustache site
45. Laughable
46. Batted first for the Rangers
48. Rubbernecked on I-10
49. Pecos River bank breaker
52. Chuy's chip dip
54. Fancy wheels for the Skyline HS prom
55. Mo. town
56. Bivouac
61. Anvil Pub pints
62. Clear
64. Cooking staple, to Rachael Ray
65. Texas Senate aide
66. Got up
67. Pickle flavoring
68. Do a Whole Foods cashier's job
69. UH Men's Chorus voice
70. Times to call, in The Comfort News classifieds

### Down (cont.)

10. Compassion
11. Resembling some UT walls
12. Star bursts
13. Dealey Plaza grassy mound
21. Zipped again, as a storage bag
25. Clunker
26. Lone Star Golf Club do-over
27. Ms. Didrikson Zaharias
28. Houston Zoo feline
29. Sea eagles
30. "Pipe down!"
32. Penpoints
34. In the thick of
36. East End Barber sound
37. South Houston HS outbreak
38. Like some dorms at TTU
41. Alicia of "Falcon Crest"
44. Stooped shoulders, e.g.
45. ___-CIO
46. Ease up
47. State park with an 84,000-acre reservoir on the Rio Grande
49. Abilene Regional Airport plane parts
50. Lubbock Master Gardeners fragrant bloom
51. SMU frat letter
53. Passover feast
55. Bed board
57. Turn over
58. Tel ___
59. UT Dermatology Clinic concern
60. Abbott and Cornyn, briefly
63. Prefix with bar

## Texas Festivals

Texas seems to have more than its fair share of festivals. No matter what time of year you visit, there's a new event to discover. Some of the country's most unique festivals can be found in the state.

As might be expected, Austin plays host to a weird festival. Each August, visitors flock to Bat Fest. This festival features live music, arts and crafts, bat costume contests, children's activities and food and drinks.

In July, the Great Texas Mosquito Festival has Clute buzzing. One highlight of this event is Willie-Man-Chew, the 25-foot inflatable mosquito. Port Aransas hosts the three-day Texas SandFest in April. The beaches of the Gulf of Mexico are turned into a toy chest of treasures as artists create amazing sculptures out of sand. Master and amateur sculptors come from across the country for this event, the U.S.'s largest native sand sculpture competition. The festival started in 1997 and contributed more than $200,000 in scholarships and donations to area nonprofits in 2017. Each year, more than 100,000 visits travel to Port Aransas to see the creative works, listen to music and take their own sculpting classes.

Music plays a role in any festival, but Texas has several events dedicated only to music. While most people have heard of SXSW (March) and Austin City Limits Music Festival (September/October), there are several others that draw thousands of fans. The Neon Desert Music Festival takes place in El Paso in May. The Downtown festival was first held in 2011 and has drawn big stars like Moby, Wiz Khalifa, Ludacris, Future and Cardi B. The River City Rockfest in San Antonio is also held in May. This heavy metal extravaganza has featured Def Leppard, the Scorpions, Anthrax and Megadeth. Houston's new Bloom Music Festival featured 50 musical performances in downtown.

Part III: Michigan Activities

Texans love their bluebonnets, so of course there are festivals celebrating the iconic flower. In Chappell Hill, the "Official State of Texas Bluebonnet Festival" takes place each April. This small town is on Highway 290 between Houston and Austin and claims to be "the heart of Bluebonnet Country." The festival features music, pony rides, shopping and more. But Chappell Hill has some competition, as Burnet ("the Bluebonnet Capital of Texas") calls its Bluebonnet Festival "the most exciting small-town festival in Texas." Ennis holds the Bluebonnet Trails Festival, while Natalia has a Bluebonnet Festival and Parade and even crowns a Bluebonnet Royal Court.

Austin City Limits Music Festival is produced by Austin-based company C3 Presents and draws in about 450,000 attendees every year.

Texas Crosswords

## Concert Venues Crossword
Solution on page 149.

### Across
1. Tyler's Barbeque kitchen cover-up
6. Heidi's home
10. Astros rivals
14. Aquarium fish
15. Author Roberts
16. Assert
17. San Antonio sports and concert venue
20. Grassy area
21. Trans-Siberian Railroad city

### Down
1. DOJ div.
2. Part of MPH
3. Texas hwy.
4. End of a threat
5. Fingered
6. Raggedy doll
7. Plumb crazy
8. On time
9. Taqueria Jalisco hot stuff
10. SMU dorm VIPs

# Part III: Michigan Activities

## Across (cont.)

22. Mega Millions drawing night
26. Cafe Madrid rice dish
31. Cry on a Six Flags roller coaster
32. Make a choice
34. Fischers Meat stamp of approval
35. Set a price of
36. Old Italian money
38. Rarely
40. Houston Symphony Orchestra home
42. "Finally!"
45. Garb
46. AOL alternative
49. Ode or haiku
50. ___ Moines
51. Approximately
52. Marble Falls daily
55. Inter-Continental Jewelers hoop
58. Mumbai Grill dress
60. Texas A&M assistance
61. Dallas performing arts facility
69. MasterCard competitor
70. Gulf port
71. Compare
72. Fill to the gills
73. "___ we forget"
74. Hoity-toity sorts

## Down (cont.)

11. Carthage st. crosser
12. "That means ___!"
13. Personal ad letters
18. Motorists' org.
19. White House nickname
22. Old DFW flyer
23. Sounds of hesitation
24. Comics shriek
25. Bygone time
27. Down time
28. "Acid"
29. Commotion
30. Texas Gov. Houston
33. Kazen Elementary School adhesive
36. ___ Saenz, Tex.
37. Bad result for a Texans QB
38. Give in to gravity
39. 1997 US Open winner
40. Door part
41. Amarillo Fire Department equipment
42. Suitable
43. Blue Jays on Globe Life Park scoreboards
44. Floral ring
46. Baylor Medical Center scan
47. Texas tax ID
48. Holiday quaff
50. Pooh-pooh
51. Decree
53. Naval letters
54. Birth-related
56. Sound at Massage Envy
57. Cambodian currency
59. Frosts, as a cake
61. Some advanced UT degs.
62. Trustpoint Hospital doc bloc
63. SAT transport
64. Computer file suffix
65. Atlanta-based station
66. Texas Golden Gloves dec.
67. Confederate soldier, for short
68. Print measures

## Texas Arts

Texas cities, particularly the larger urban areas of Dallas, Houston and Austin, are home to countless art and cultural attractions.

At the top of any "must see" list is the Dallas Museum of Art. This collection of 23,000+ works is one of the largest art museums in the U.S. It covers 5,000 years of history and visitors can see a great variety of works. Some of the most popular artists include Jackson Pollock, Edward Hopper, Winslow Homer and Grant Wood. The museum also has an incredible selection of Texas art—works inspired by Texas or created by Texas artists. Next door is the Nasher Sculpture Center. This museum houses Raymond and Patsy Nasher's incredible sculptures, which they began collecting in the 1950s. The collection is extensive and covers everything from traditional works by Auguste Rodin to modern masterpieces by Joan Miró and Pablo Picasso. Other artists include Alexander Calder and his signature mobiles, Paul Gauguin, Willem de Kooning, Henry Moore, and David Smith.

Visitors could spend days viewing Houston's array of arts offerings. The city's Museum District has nearly 20 museums, including the Museum of Fine Arts, Houston, the Menil Collection, the Houston Museum of Natural Science and the Children's Museum of Houston.

Houstonians can thank art collectors John and Dominique de Menil for many of their attractions. The Menil Collection is a 30-acre campus of art consisting of several buildings. The once private collection includes paintings, sculptures, drawings, prints, antiquities, photographs, rare books and more. Among the more than 17,000 works are pieces by Max Ernst, Man Ray, Andy Warhol, and Henri Matisse.

Another popular destination is the Rothko Chapel. The building is not only a non-denominational chapel, but also a meditation and meeting hall—but mostly a destination for modern art lovers. The walls are lined with 14 paintings by American artist Mark Rothko. The de

Part III: Michigan Activities

Menils commissioned the abstract expressionist to create the chapel in 1964. The black paintings fill the octagon-shaped building. Outside is a reflecting pool and Barnett Newman's Broken Obelisk sculpture, a tribute to Dr. Martin Luther King Jr.

In Austin, the University of Texas is home to the Blanton Museum of Art. Founded in 1963, this museum's has a permanent collection of nearly 18,000 works. Visitors can enjoy everything from modern and contemporary pieces to Old Master paintings. The museum has a one of the largest collections of Latin American art in the US.

Some of Blanton's most unexpected pieces are by (or focused on) a Texan known for her beauty, not her artistic abilities. Farrah Fawcett was a student of UT professor Charles Umlauf in the 1960s. Umlauf, a life drawing and sculpture professor, became the actress' mentor and lifelong friend. Over the years, Fawcett gathered an impressive collection of Umlauf works, including some sculptures of her as his muse. Through the years, Umlauf continued to support Fawcett's interest in sculpting and painting. When Fawcett died in 2009, she left a large portion of her art collection to the Blanton. These include some of her own pieces, including 15 hydrastone works she did of her torso and a bust of her older sister Diane. There is also a drawing of Fawcett's eye that Andy Warhol did on a napkin.

A much larger collection of Umlauf's works can be seen at the Umlauf Sculpture Garden & Museum near Zilker Park.

Thanks to the LANDMARKS Public Art Program, Austin visitors never know where they will find amazing pieces of art. This program has installed more than three dozen works outdoors and in academic buildings on the UT campus.

Other top-notch Texas destinations for art include the Amarillo Museum of Art, which is hope to four Georgia O'Keeffe works; Beaumont's Art Museum of Southeast Texas, which has a superb collection of Texas pieces; and Fort Worth's Kimbell Art Museum, which houses Michelangelo's first known painting, *The Torment of Saint Anthony*.

The Dallas Museum of Arts is housed in a building designed by Edward Larrabee Barnes, a winner of the American Institute of Architects Gold Medal.

Courtesy of Carol M. Highsmith via the Library of Congress

# Texas Crosswords

## Colleges Crossword

Solution on page 149.

### Across

1. Back muscles, in TSU gym
5. Castle defense
9. Way up the UT clock tower
14. TCU orchestra composer
15. Singer Guthrie
16. Ditto
17. Ditto
18. "Don't go!"
19. SMU art supporter
20. Paxton and Abbott, briefly

### Down

1. Weight abbr.
2. Battery size
3. Channel for film buffs
4. Bundle
5. Elements Massage worker
6. Food scrap
7. Jai ___
8. Chihuahua, e.g.
9. Silvery fish
10. The Cultured Cup buy

# Part III: Michigan Activities

### Across (cont.)
22. Matinee ___
24. Baylor pay stub abbr.
25. Exempt, in a way
29. Like a KLBK newscast
31. Lyndon Johnson dog
32. Lubbock Power & Light problem
34. "___ the night before…"
38. 401(k) alternative
39. Astral Catering coffee dispensers
40. Texas National Guard command
42. Snitch
44. Texas A&M scholarship money
46. Let down, as hair
47. Slow partner
49. Shakespeare's river
51. Wyo. neighbor
52. Cruz and Daffan
53. Made good as new at Sylvie Alterations
55. Asian New Year
56. Diplomat's skill
58. Conjecture
60. Owns
63. Satisfied sounds
65. Some military hospitals, initially
66. Hate
68. Film ___
70. Radio tuner
74. Threw a football at Rice Stadium
75. Wight, for one
76. Numerical prefix
77. New Light Christian Church tither's amount
78. Whispers sweet nothings
79. The Expanse airer

### Down (cont.)
11. Crafts website
12. Allison Hedge Coke, e.g.
13. Eaton Realty's sign of success
21. Fall stopper
23. 4-F's opposite
25. Craving
26. Make fizzy
27. Like a Jessica Drake film
28. Sicilian mount
30. Powerful engine
33. Golden Wok cuisine
35. Yellowstone sight
36. Roxie Theatre Company parenthetical comments
37. John Cornyn's workplace
41. Arctic plain
43. Brewer's kiln
45. Movie formats
48. Corsicana pool site
50. Bodies of work
54. Italian or Irish
57. Cry of exasperation
59. Windows predecessor
60. Dagger handle
61. Up to it
62. Cold-shoulder
64. C-worthy
67. Hamilton's prov.
69. UN workers' grp.
71. Like some Texas roads in the winter
72. DOJ division
73. Not of the cloth

# Texas Crosswords

## Playhouse Sudoku

Use logic to fill in the boxes so every row, column and 3x3 box contains the letters P–L–A–Y–H–O–U–S–E, in honor of the University Playhouse at Texas A&M. Solution on page 150.

|   |   |   |   |   |   |   |   |   |
|---|---|---|---|---|---|---|---|---|
| L |   | P |   |   |   |   |   | A |
|   | H |   | U |   |   |   | O |   |
|   |   |   |   | E |   |   |   | L |
|   |   |   | H |   | E |   | L |   |
|   |   | U |   |   |   | Y |   |   |
|   | E |   | P |   | S |   |   |   |
| E |   |   |   | S |   |   |   |   |
|   | O |   |   |   | Y |   | P |   |
| Y |   |   |   |   |   | E |   | U |

## MFAH Rearranged

The Museum of Fine Arts, Houston, houses more than 65,000 works of art. It is commonly referred to as the MFAH. The letters M-F-A-H can be arranged to form 24 different combinations. Here are 21 of those combinations. Which three are missing? Solution on page 150.

| MAFH | HFAM | AFMH |
| HMAF | MFHA | HAMF |
| AHMF | AMHF | MFAH |
| FAHM | FHAM | AMFH |
| HAFM | HFMA | FMHA |
| MAHF | MHAF | HMFA |
| AFHM | FHMA | FMAH |

Part III: Michigan Activities

# Texas History

The Spaniards claimed Texas in 1519, but did not arrive until the 18th century. At the time of their "discovery," the land was populated by Native Americans, who had been there for more than 10,000 years. The Spanish built many missions in Texas in hopes of spreading the Catholic religion to the Native Americans and securing the land for Spain.

From 1519 to 1848, five countries – Spain, France, Mexico, the Republic of Texas and the United States – tried to claim the land. Mexico won its independence from Spain in 1821 and Texas became part of Mexico. Many settlers, led by Stephen F. Austin, arrived the following year. Austin called a meeting with Mexico in 1833 due to Texans' increasing discontent with the country. The meeting did not go well, and Austin was arrested. This eventually led to the Texas Revolution in 1835. The most famous battle was at the Alamo Mission in 1836. Mexican President Antonio Lopez de Santa Anna led his large army to the Alamo and, during a 13-day siege, killed all 200 Texians defending the mission. "Remember the Alamo!" became a famous cry, and Santa Anna's cruelty inspired Texians to sign up for the army. Shortly thereafter, the Mexicans were defeated on April 21, 1936 at the battle of San Jacinto.

General Sam Houston was elected president and the city of Austin became the capital three years later. In 1845, Texas became part of the United States. During the Civil War, Texas became part of the Confederacy, despite now Governor Sam Houston's resistance. Houston was removed from office and replaced by Lieutenant Governor Edward Clark. In the late 1860s, Texas was full of cotton fields and cattle ranches. Then oil struck – first discovered at Corsicana in 1894, then at Spindletop in 1901. In 1930, the East Texas Oil Field was discovered and Texas was forever changed.

Texas has experience numerous natural disasters, including two devastating hurricanes. Galveston was hit by a hurricane in 1900 that

# Texas Crosswords

killed thousands of people. And Hurricane Harvey in 2017 was one of the costliest storms in history, causing at least $125 billion in damage in the Houston area.

Texas, like the rest of the country, was hit hard during the depression of the 1930s. But the state rebounded after World War II and in the 1950s and 1960s. Dallas was a horrific scene on November 22, 1963, when President John F. Kennedy was assassinated as his motorcade drove through downtown. Texas native Lyndon Johnson was sworn in as the 36th president aboard Air Force One at Love Field.

The world's first domed stadium, the Astrodome, opened in Houston in 1965. Often called the "Eighth Wonder of the World," the Astrodome was home to the Houston Astros and Houston Oilers. The Astrodome also hosted the Houston Livestock Show and Rodeo for many years and was the setting of the Battle of the Sexes, the legendary match between Billie Jean King and Bobby Riggs.

In 1961, the Manned Spacecraft Center opened in Houston. Eventually becoming the Johnson Space Center, it is the Mission Control for all space flights. All eyes were on the space center on July 20, 1969, when flight control helped Neil Armstrong and Buzz Aldrin land on the moon and return home safe.

Texas, of course, continues to thrive today. With a population of more than 28 million, it is the second-largest state in the nation. The Lone Star state has been transforming from a more rural state to one that is urban and high-tech. "Silicon Hills" (Austin) and "Silicon Prairie" (north Dallas) are up-and-coming areas, and Texas is the headquarters of several technology companies, including Dell, Texas Instruments and AT&T.

The state has numerous top-notch universities and many elite medical and medical research centers. Major companies include Exxon Mobil, Phillips 66, Valero Energy, American Airlines, Kimberly-Clark, Whole Foods Market and Tenet Healthcare.

The last stand at the Alamo, led by Davy Crockett and James Bowie, gave birth to the refrain "Remeber the Alamo," a battle cry during the Mexican-American War.

*Courtesy of Carol M. Highsmith via the Library of Congress*

Part III: Michigan Activities

# Texas Time Line

Match the event with the year that it happened. Answers on page 150.

1682
1766
1832
1845
1883
1917
1954
1960
1963
2001

1. First Spanish mission was created.
2. Texas became a state.
3. President John F. Kennedy was assassinated at Dallas.
4. Women gained the right to serve on Texas juries.
5. First recorded hurricane to hit Texas.
6. Enron filed for bankruptcy.
7. Texas Revolution began.
8. Gov. James Ferguson impeached and convicted.
9. University of Texas established.
10. Dallas Cowboys founded.

# Texas Crosswords

# History Crossword

Solution on page 150.

## Across

1. Arlington Chess Club piece
5. Proficient
9. Saturated
15. Biblical outcast
16. What a rodeo bronco may do
17. Show up
18. 44-Across Mexican general
20. 44-Across Texas commander
21. Make a choice
22. 36th POTUS

## Down

1. Mexican moolah
2. PDQ
3. Texas: "Say What You ___"
4. Cowboys fanatic
5. Bridled Passion Farm horses
6. Movie pooch
7. PC linkup
8. Astros stats
9. Nymph chaser
10. Bruins legend

# Part III: Michigan Activities

## Across (cont.)

23. Hog heaven
25. Amarillo Hair Salon stock
26. Desert haven
28. Approximately
30. Spills the beans
33. Rocky hill
35. 1300 hrs.
39. Sleek, in car lingo
40. John Sealy Hospital treatment
43. Wish otherwise
44. Texas Army rally cry and song title
47. Green prefix
48. Purposeful
49. Caesar's "vidi"
50. Shoulder gesture
52. "No ___" (menu phrase)
53. Salad green
54. Houston shuttle org.
56. Pack leader
59. "Butt out!," initially
62. Star of Texas B&B, e.g.
64. Texas bond rating
65. DPD alert, for short
68. 44-Across songwriter
70. First singer to record 44-Across
73. Meeting slate
74. "Let it stand"
75. Baylor frat letter
76. Rockport Beach wear
77. Austin's 6th Street establishments
78. Comic book mutants

## Down (cont.)

11. Game of Thrones menace
12. Texas Swimming Center plunge
13. Wicked
14. Loch ___ monster
19. "Woe is me!"
24. Chabad Lubavitch of El Paso scrolls
26. Brownsville's Symphony in the Park woodwind
27. Backs of boats on Lake Whitney
29. Kind of bean
30. Uncovers
31. Bloodsucker
32. Houston SWAT protection
34. Salsa brand
36. Rub out
37. Selena Gomez shoes
38. Kilgore Animal Control cat calls
40. KLTV schedule abbr.
41. Longhorns football coach
42. Gov. Abbott's Pancake
45. Texas Lottery game: ___ Millions
46. Old Italian bread
51. Straighten
53. World Blend tea order
55. Rope fiber
57. Less strict
58. Baumann Auto Repair bill costs
59. SMU bus. degs.
60. Lake Highlands YMCA class
61. Actor Wilson
63. Accident investigation agcy.
65. Rice physics class study
66. Hot sauce: Texas ___
67. Cereal grain
69. Nutritional std.
71. SAT flight info
72. AT&T Center box office

Texas Crosswords

## Counties Word Search

Solution on page 150.

```
Y W O K H S T A R R S J K T Q
Z A V A L A N I N O T N L O O
E D V E A E N Z T Y G Q T W F
U E I J E D O V V U C K B T Q
N L G W R G X N M D S N C Y W
N T U A K E R R Q A S A S A L
C A W A R C H E R I S L J L J
X T H B U Z F S N K L O O C D
S X H F Y D A X W A Y N N P K
S U P T O N Y G F A G W B L I
F I J F T X I D N G I X O T H
U S L C A S S Y B U W P J F A
Q C N L S G Q Y R E O M D A W
B O R D E N H A L E L Y R W V
S O G L U R E L Y T N L L V Y
```

| | | |
|---|---|---|
| ARCHER | GARZA | REAL |
| BELL | HALE | STARR |
| BORDEN | JACK | TITUS |
| CASS | KERR | TYLER |
| CLAY | LEON | UPTON |
| DELTA | MASON | WARD |
| ELLIS | NOLAN | YOUNG |
| FALLS | POLK | ZAVALA |

Answer Key

Texas Crosswords

# Part I

### Famous Texans Crossword (page 4)

### Martin Sudoku (page 6)

### Astronauts Word Search (page 4)

### Infamous Texans Crossword (page 8)

### Wiley Post Sudoku (page 6)

### Actors Crossword (page 12)

Morgan Fairchild

138

# Answer Key

## Murphy Sudoku (page 14)

| M | P | R | Y | H | U |
|---|---|---|---|---|---|
| Y | H | U | M | P | R |
| U | R | H | P | Y | M |
| P | Y | M | U | R | H |
| R | M | P | H | U | Y |
| H | U | Y | R | M | P |

## TV News Crossword (page 16)

## Liza Koshy Sudoku (page 14)

| I | Z | K | S | O | H | Y | A | L |
|---|---|---|---|---|---|---|---|---|
| H | L | O | A | Y | Z | S | K | I |
| A | Y | S | I | K | L | H | O | Z |
| Y | S | A | L | H | O | Z | I | K |
| L | K | H | Z | A | I | O | S | Y |
| O | I | Z | Y | S | K | A | L | H |
| Z | A | Y | K | I | S | L | H | O |
| S | O | I | H | L | Y | K | Z | A |
| K | H | L | O | Z | A | I | Y | S |

## Country Music Crossword (page 20)

## Stunt Doubles (page 15)

1. JOHN HAWKES;
2. KATHY BAKER;
3. MARY MARTIN;
4. JIM PARSONS;
5. SARAH SHAHI;
6. MARTHA HYER;
7. JOAN CROAWFORD;
8. GINGER ROGERS;
9. VALERIE PERRINE;
10. DEBBIE REYNOLDS;
11. FOREST WHITAKER;
12. JENNIFER GARNER.

## Buck Owens Sudoku (page 22)

| U | O | S | C | W | K | B | E | N |
|---|---|---|---|---|---|---|---|---|
| C | W | E | B | U | N | S | K | O |
| N | B | K | O | E | S | W | C | U |
| K | N | O | W | B | E | C | U | S |
| S | C | B | N | K | U | O | W | E |
| W | E | U | S | O | C | N | B | K |
| E | S | N | U | C | B | K | O | W |
| B | K | W | E | N | O | U | S | C |
| O | U | C | K | S | W | E | N | B |

139

# Texas Crosswords

## Joplin Sudoku (page 22)

| N | O | L | I | J | P |
|---|---|---|---|---|---|
| I | P | J | L | O | N |
| O | L | P | J | N | I |
| J | N | I | P | L | O |
| L | I | O | N | P | J |
| P | J | N | O | I | L |

## Jordan Sudoku (page 28)

| R | D | A | N | O | J |
|---|---|---|---|---|---|
| O | J | N | R | D | A |
| D | R | J | A | N | O |
| N | A | O | J | R | D |
| A | O | R | D | J | N |
| J | N | D | O | A | R |

## Star Crossed (page 23)

1. LYLE LOVETT;
2. GEORGE STRAIT;
3. KENNY ROGERS;
4. SELENA GOMEZ;
5. MEAT LOAF;
6. CLINT BLACK.

## Cryptic Quote (page 29)

"PEOPLE WHO WORRY ABOUT THEIR HAIR ALL THE TIME, FRANKLY, ARE BORING."

## Women Crossword (page 26)

## Politicians Crossword (page 32)

## Dworaczyk Sudoku (page 28)

| Z | A | Y | D | C | O | W | R | K |
|---|---|---|---|---|---|---|---|---|
| R | W | D | K | A | Z | Y | C | O |
| C | O | K | R | W | Y | A | D | Z |
| D | Y | R | O | K | W | C | Z | A |
| A | Z | W | C | Y | D | O | K | R |
| O | K | C | A | Z | R | D | Y | W |
| K | D | Z | Y | O | A | R | W | C |
| W | R | O | Z | D | C | K | A | Y |
| Y | C | A | W | R | K | Z | O | D |

## Who Am I? Sudoku (page 34)

| E | C | L | O | A | T | K | S | D |
|---|---|---|---|---|---|---|---|---|
| T | O | K | E | D | S | C | A | L |
| D | A | S | K | L | C | O | E | T |
| C | L | E | A | T | O | S | D | K |
| ▶ S | T | O | C | K | D | A | L | E |
| K | D | A | S | E | L | T | O | C |
| L | K | C | D | O | A | E | T | S |
| O | E | T | L | S | K | D | C | A |
| A | S | D | T | C | E | L | K | O |

# Answer Key

## Austin Sudoku (page 34)

| N | U | T | I | S | A |
|---|---|---|---|---|---|
| A | I | S | N | T | U |
| T | A | U | S | I | N |
| I | S | N | U | A | T |
| U | T | I | A | N | S |
| S | N | A | T | U | I |

## Howard Sudoku (page 40)

| O | D | A | R | H | W |
|---|---|---|---|---|---|
| H | R | W | D | O | A |
| W | H | D | A | R | O |
| R | A | O | W | D | H |
| D | W | H | O | A | R |
| A | O | R | H | W | D |

## Senators Word Search (page 35)

## What's in a Name (page 41)

1. a;   4. f;   7. i;   9. e;
2. c;   5. g;   8. j;   10. b.
3. d;   6. h;

Bonus: DESIGN PROF

## Business Fill-in (page 43)
FRITO-LAY.

## Authors Crossword (page 38)

## Drop Down Quote (page 43)

"EVERY MAN HAS HIS PRICE, OR A GUY LIKE ME COULDN'T EXIST."

## Title Box (page 40)
LOVE BEYOND REASON

| 7 | 6 | 5 | 16 |
|---|---|---|----|
| 8 | 1 | 4 | 15 |
| 9 | 2 | 3 | 14 |
| 10 | 11 | 12 | 13 |

## Industrialists Crossword (page 44)

| P | A | P | A |   | S | M | A | S | H |   | S | C | O | T |
|---|---|---|---|---|---|---|---|---|---|---|---|---|---|---|
| D | E | L | L |   | E | A | G | E | R |   | O | R | C | A |
| F | R | O | M |   | T | R | U | E | S |   | F | O | A | L |
| S | O | Y | S | A | U | C | E |   | A | T | O | L | L |   |
|   |   |   | C | P | U |   | M | A | R | Y | K | A | Y |   |
| H | O | G | A | N |   | S | K | I | L | L |   |   |   |   |
| U | N | D | I | E | S |   | O | L | I | O |   | T | A | S |
| B | E | A | L |   | P | E | R | O | T |   | H | U | N | T |
| S | A | Y |   | O | O | Z | E |   | O | W | E | S | T | O |
|   |   |   | T | O | R | A | H |   | U | L | T |   |   |   |
| F | I | O | R | I | N | A |   | A | S | K | E | W |   |   |
| E | M | M | Y | S |   | A | G | I | T | A | T | E | D |   |
| L | O | A | D |   | S | O | P | H | S |   | F | R | A | Y |
| T | U | N | E |   | A | S | S | E | T |   | R | I | C | E |
| S | T | I | R |   | G | U | E | S | S |   | O | O | H | S |

141

# Texas Crosswords

## Businesses Crossword (page 46)

## Athletes Crossword (page 52)

## Companies Word Search (page 48)

## A. J. Foyt Sudoku (page 54)

| O | Y | J | T | A | F |
|---|---|---|---|---|---|
| T | A | F | O | Y | J |
| J | O | Y | F | T | A |
| F | T | A | Y | J | O |
| A | F | T | J | O | Y |
| Y | J | O | A | F | T |

## Knight Moves (page 51)

| 18 | 59 | 50 | *1* | 48 | 15 | 22 | 63 |
|----|----|----|----|----|----|----|----|
| 51 | 2 | 17 | 60 | 21 | 64 | 47 | 14 |
| 58 | 19 | 4 | 49 | 16 | 23 | 62 | 45 |
| 3 | 52 | 57 | 20 | 61 | 46 | 13 | 24 |
| 34 | 5 | 40 | 53 | 36 | 25 | 44 | 11 |
| 39 | 56 | 35 | 8 | 41 | 12 | 29 | 26 |
| 6 | 33 | 54 | 37 | 28 | 31 | 10 | 43 |
| 55 | 38 | 7 | 32 | 9 | 42 | 27 | 30 |

## Dez Bryant Sudoku (page 54)

| E | D | Z | B | A | Y | N | R | T |
|---|---|---|---|---|---|---|---|---|
| R | B | Y | N | T | Z | D | A | E |
| N | T | A | R | E | D | Z | Y | B |
| Z | E | T | A | D | N | Y | B | R |
| Y | R | D | T | Z | B | E | N | A |
| B | A | N | Y | R | E | T | Z | D |
| T | Z | R | D | Y | A | B | E | N |
| A | Y | B | E | N | T | R | D | Z |
| D | N | E | Z | B | R | A | T | Y |

142

# Answer Key

## Dallas Cowboys Word Search (page 55)

## Texas Rangers Word Search (page 60)

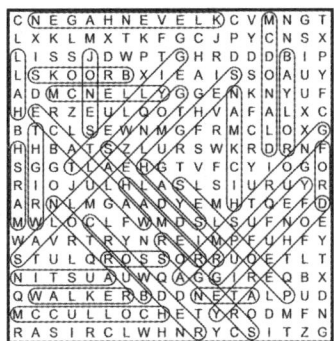

## Sports Crossword (page 56)

## Texas Athletes Hodgepodge (page 58)

Cowboys: AIKMAN, DORSETT, EL-LIOTT, HENDERSON, LILLY, STAUBACH
Astros: ALTUVE, BERKMAN, BIGGIO, CEDENO, SPRINGER
Longhorns: CAMPBELL, LAYNE, MCCOY; NOBIS
Spurs: ERVIN, GILMORE, ROBINSON
Olympians: PATTERSON, SWOOPES
Boxer: FOREMAN
Hidden Name: BABE DIDRIKSON ZAHARIAS.

143

Texas Crosswords

# Part II

## Panhandle Crossword (page 66)

| T | H | A | I | | C | U | F | F | S | | L | A | D | S |
|---|---|---|---|---|---|---|---|---|---|---|---|---|---|---|
| D | A | M | N | | D | A | L | A | I | | I | C | E | T |
| S | W | A | K | | S | W | O | R | D | | P | U | C | E |
| | R | Y | E | | | G | R | E | W | | M | A | R | |
| M | A | I | | S | N | O | | A | B | I | L | E | N | E |
| A | F | L | | L | Y | N | C | H | | L | E | N | T | O |
| Y | E | L | P | | M | E | A | | B | L | T | | | |
| A | W | O | L | | P | A | M | P | A | | | O | H | O |
| | | U | G | H | | E | A | R | | N | E | H | I | |
| A | L | A | M | O | | S | O | R | R | Y | | R | M | N |
| L | U | B | B | O | C | K | | E | E | R | | E | S | T |
| E | L | S | | F | O | A | M | | | S | P | F | | |
| P | L | U | G | | U | T | U | R | N | | I | O | N | S |
| P | E | R | U | | R | E | T | R | O | | E | R | S | T |
| O | D | D | S | | T | R | E | S | S | | D | D | A | Y |

## One and Only One Vega (page 69)

| V | G | E | A | E | V | V | G | A | E | V | E | G | E | V |
|---|---|---|---|---|---|---|---|---|---|---|---|---|---|---|
| E | G | A | V | G | E | A | V | E | G | G | E | V | A | E |
| G | A | E | V | E | A | G | E | E | G | V | E | G | V | G |
| V | E | G | G | A | E | V | G | G | A | V | A | G | V | E |
| V | E | G | G | V | V | E | G | E | V | G | E | V | G | A |
| E | G | A | V | E | G | E | G | A | V | E | G | G | A | E |
| V | G | E | A | A | A | G | G | G | E | E | E | V | V | V |
| E | V | G | A | V | G | G | E | E | V | E | E | G | E | E |
| G | E | E | V | G | A | G | V | E | A | G | V | A | G | V |
| E | V | G | A | G | E | G | A | A | A | G | E | A | E | A |
| V | A | G | A | G | G | E | A | A | V | G | E | E | G | V |
| E | A | G | G | A | V | V | A | E | E | G | A | G | E | G |
| G | V | E | V | V | A | V | V | A | V | E | V | E | A | E |
| V | A | G | E | E | V | G | A | E | V | V | G | A | V | E |
| E | V | E | A | E | G | S | R | G | S | E | V | G | E | V |

## Athens Sudoku (page 68)

| S | N | H | T | E | A |
|---|---|---|---|---|---|
| T | E | A | N | S | H |
| N | H | T | E | A | S |
| E | A | S | H | N | T |
| A | T | N | S | H | E |
| H | S | E | A | T | N |

## Southland Sudoku (page 72)

| O | D | N | T | U | H | L | S | A |
|---|---|---|---|---|---|---|---|---|
| T | U | S | L | O | A | N | H | D |
| A | L | H | D | S | N | U | T | O |
| H | A | D | U | L | S | T | O | N |
| N | T | L | A | H | O | D | U | S |
| U | S | O | N | D | T | A | L | H |
| S | N | A | O | T | L | H | D | U |
| L | H | U | S | A | D | O | N | T |
| D | O | T | H | N | U | S | A | L |

## Munday Sudoku (page 68)

| M | D | A | Y | N | U |
|---|---|---|---|---|---|
| Y | N | U | D | A | M |
| A | U | M | N | Y | D |
| N | Y | D | U | M | A |
| U | M | N | A | D | Y |
| D | A | Y | M | U | N |

## Dallas Crossword (page 72)

| N | A | S | A | | K | A | G | A | N | | S | C | A | G |
|---|---|---|---|---|---|---|---|---|---|---|---|---|---|---|
| B | L | O | C | | A | R | O | M | A | | H | A | T | E |
| C | E | L | L | | H | U | G | E | R | | I | S | B | N |
| | | | A | U | D | U | B | O | N | C | E | N | T | E | R |
| F | D | R | | A | N | A | | | | V | E | R | S | E |
| G | E | I | S | H | A | | S | A | R | I | | O | T | S |
| S | T | U | N | | | P | A | L | A | T | E | | | |
| | | | M | U | S | E | U | M | O | F | A | R | T | |
| | | | B | A | L | L | O | T | | | G | E | E | Z |
| S | P | A | | L | O | L | A | | S | P | O | N | G | E |
| E | R | I | C | A | | | P | O | E | | | E | O | N |
| W | O | R | L | D | A | Q | U | A | R | I | U | M | | |
| A | B | B | A | | L | U | N | G | E | | R | E | P | S |
| G | E | A | R | | M | I | T | E | S | | G | N | A | T |
| E | D | G | E | | S | P | O | R | T | | E | T | S | Y |

144

# Answer Key

## East Texas Crossword (page 76)

## People from Houston Word Search (page 79)

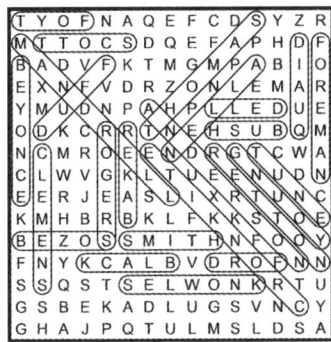

## Fairmount Sudoku (page 78)

| M | R | F | N | T | A | U | I | O |
|---|---|---|---|---|---|---|---|---|
| A | U | N | I | O | F | R | M | T |
| I | O | T | R | U | M | A | N | F |
| T | I | M | O | R | U | F | A | N |
| N | A | U | T | F | I | O | R | M |
| R | F | O | A | M | N | T | U | I |
| O | M | A | U | N | T | I | F | R |
| F | T | I | M | A | R | N | O | U |
| U | N | R | F | I | O | M | T | A |

## City Grid (page 80)

## Shifted Fairmount Sudoku (page 78)

| F | I | T | R | M | O | A | U | N |
|---|---|---|---|---|---|---|---|---|
| R | A | M | U | T | N | F | I | O |
| U | N | I | F | O | M | T | A | R |
| O | M | F | I | R | U | N | T | A |
| M | T | R | N | A | F | U | O | I |
| I | O | U | A | N | T | M | R | F |
| A | R | N | T | U | I | O | F | M |
| T | F | O | M | I | A | R | N | U |
| N | U | A | O | F | R | I | M | T |

## Texas Building Blocks (page 82)

1. SPRING;
2. RINGS;
3. SING;
4. GIN;
5. IN;
6. N.

## Houston Astros All-Stars Word Search (page 83)

145

# Texas Crosswords

## South Texas Crossword (page 86)

| S | E | R | E | ■ | P | C | K | E | Y | ■ | W | H | E | E |
|---|---|---|---|---|---|---|---|---|---|---|---|---|---|---|
| P | L | A | T | ■ | L | A | R | G | E | ■ | H | I | L | L |
| L | P | G | A | ■ | O | N | I | O | N | ■ | U | G | L | I |
| E | A | G | L | E | P | A | S | S | ■ | M | P | H | ■ | ■ |
| E | S | E | ■ | A | S | P | ■ | ■ | B | A | S | S | E | T |
| N | O | D | A | T | ■ | E | M | B | E | R | ■ | P | T | A |
| ■ | ■ | ■ | C | U | P | ■ | E | A | R | ■ | P | O | U | T |
| ■ | C | O | R | P | U | S | C | H | R | I | S | T | I | ■ |
| L | O | V | E | ■ | P | E | C | ■ | Y | R | S | ■ | ■ | ■ |
| A | L | E | ■ | P | I | X | A | R | ■ | A | T | L | A | S |
| C | A | R | P | A | L | ■ | ■ | O | A | T | ■ | A | N | I |
| ■ | ■ | L | A | Y | ■ | G | A | L | V | E | S | T | O | N |
| S | W | A | T | ■ | L | I | S | L | E | ■ | E | I | R | E |
| A | I | N | T | ■ | P | R | I | O | R | ■ | G | N | A | W |
| T | I | D | Y | ■ | S | L | A | N | T | ■ | O | A | K | Y |

## Edinburg Sudoku (page 90)

| E | R | B | I | G | D | U | N |
|---|---|---|---|---|---|---|---|
| D | U | N | G | I | E | R | B |
| U | G | I | E | B | R | N | D |
| R | B | D | N | U | G | I | E |
| I | D | R | U | E | N | B | G |
| N | E | G | B | R | I | D | U |
| G | I | U | D | N | B | E | R |
| B | N | E | R | D | U | G | I |

## Combes Sudoku (page 88)

| E | O | M | C | S | B |
|---|---|---|---|---|---|
| B | S | C | O | M | E |
| M | C | S | B | E | O |
| O | B | E | M | C | S |
| C | E | B | S | O | M |
| S | M | O | E | B | C |

## Cities Word Search (page 90)

| U | P | J | A | L | J | W | A | C | O | P | L | A | N | O |
|---|---|---|---|---|---|---|---|---|---|---|---|---|---|---|
| A | S | A | N | A | N | T | O | N | I | O | D | W | H | K |
| Z | W | N | F | O | R | T | W | O | R | T | H | Q | H | U |
| S | K | E | X | N | E | E | L | L | I | K | E | K | O | L |
| J | I | D | G | O | L | U | B | B | O | C | K | C | M | A |
| F | V | A | A | S | B | M | C | K | I | N | N | E | Y | R |
| R | J | S | R | A | R | L | I | N | G | T | O | N | G | E |
| I | S | A | L | L | A | D | Q | J | M | L | S | D | L | D |
| S | I | P | A | E | Z | W | S | C | A | T | E | P | A | O |
| C | R | V | N | K | G | P | K | W | T | G | A | G | Q | X |
| O | V | W | D | Y | Z | L | N | O | T | S | U | O | H | Q |
| W | I | A | M | A | R | I | L | L | O | U | C | Q | R | K |
| F | N | C | O | R | P | U | S | C | H | R | I | S | T | I |
| F | G | R | A | N | D | P | R | A | I | R | I | E | M | Z |
| S | Z | K | D | A | U | S | T | I | N | Z | B | C | C | J |

## Twin Counties (page 89)

1. DIMMIT, LA SALLE;
2. STARR, CAMERON;
3. WILLACY, ZAPATA;
4. HIDALGO, KENEDY;
5. BROOKS, REFUGIO;
6. JACKSON, CALHOUN;
7. WEBB, MAVERICK;
8. LIVE OAK, GOLIAD.

## Falcon Wordsmith (page 91)

CON, CALF, FOCAL, FALCON, CALO, FON, FAN, CAN, LAC, FANO, CLAN, LOAF, FLACON, CLON, LOAN, FLAN, COAL, LOCA, FLOC, COL, OAF, FOAL, COLA, OCA.

# Answer Key

## Central Texas Crossword (page 94)

|   |   |   |   |   |   |   |   |   |   |   |   |   |
|---|---|---|---|---|---|---|---|---|---|---|---|---|
| T | U | T |   | E | M | M | A |   | A | B | O | R | T |
| E | V | E |   | N | E | E | D |   | R | U | B | I | E | S |
| S | E | A | W | O | R | L | D |   | C | R | A | V | A | T |
| L | A | T | H |   | I | D | O | L |   | S | M | E | L | L |
| A | S | S | I | G | N |   | N | E | C | T | A | R |
|   |   |   | S | M | O | G |   | T | A | S |   | W | A | R |
| D | E | L | T | A |   | A | C | I | D |   | C | A | N | E |
| E | X | A | L | T |   | S | A | T |   | V | O | L | T | A |
| N | A | V | E |   | W | E | B | B |   | I | N | K | E | D |
| T | M | I |   | O | O | O |   | E | P | I | C |
|   |   | L | O | C | K | U | P |   | L | I | E | S | I | N |
| H | A | L | V | E |   | S | A | V | E |   | A | N | N | A |
| O | R | I | E | L | S |   | S | I | X | F | L | A | G | S |
| P | A | T | R | O | L |   | H | O | U | R |   | G | O | T |
|   | B | A | T | T | Y |   | A | L | S | O |   | S | T | Y |

## Missing T–R–O–Y (page 96)

1. FROSTY;
2. NOTARY;
3. OUTCRY;
4. THEORY;
5. YOGURT;
6. TROPHY;
7. OYSTER;
8. POETRY;
9. SPORTY;
10. STORY.

Bonus: DESTROY.

## Find the Words (page 98)

CODER, CODERS, CODES, CODON, CODONS, CONDO, CONDOR, CONDORES, CONDORS, CONTO, CONTOS, COONS, COWHERD, COWHERDS, COWHERD, DONOR, DONORS, DOORS, DRESS, HERDS, HERON, HERONS, HOSED, HOSER, HOSES, NODES, ODORS, OTTOS, REDON, REDONS, RESHOT, RESHOW, RESHOWN, RESHOWS, RESOW, RESOWN, RODES, RONDE, RONDO, ROODS, SHEDS, SHERD, SHERDS, SHOTT, SHOWN, SHOWS, SNOOD, SNOOT, SNORE, SNORED, SNORES, SWOON, TONDO, TOONS, TOSHES, TOSSED, TOSSER, TOWNS, WHOSE, WONDER, WONDERS, WOODS.

## Famous Austinites Word Search (page 97)

|   |   |   |   |   |   |   |   |   |   |   |   |   |
|---|---|---|---|---|---|---|---|---|---|---|---|---|
| I | O | J | N | P | W | M | S | R | G | K | R | L | W | N |
| D | B | B | D | G | Y | J | I | O | O | N | L | K | M | C |
| T | R | O | G | A | N | C | J | K | N | I | K | C | I | C |
| T | N | O | S | N | H | O | J | N | Z | L | C | I | L | O |
| E | V | O | R | A | O | D | H | X | A | P | O | D | S | S |
| C | U | A | R | N | N | R | T | H | L | O | L | D | O | E |
| W | V | D | U | U | H | W | T | Z | E | J | L | O | N | E |
| A | S | T | Q | G | H | E | O | S | S | V | U | R | D | R |
| F | K | O | U | K | H | P | N | R | M | X | B | E | X | B |
| R | A | T | H | E | R | A | B | R | B | R | L | G | W | Z |
| W | A | L | L | A | C | H | N | K | Y | L | A | A | A | W |
| C | H | J | L | E | I | S | I | K | F | E | O | Q | I | O |
| U | Z | S | E | T | I | H | W | R | O | H | A | W | K | E |
| N | E | L | L | Y | F | N | A | D | R | O | J | W | Y | Q |
| R | E | K | L | A | W | J | L | D | D | E | I | X | A | Q |

147

Texas Crosswords

### San Antonio Word Search
(page 99)

### Colleges Word Search
(page 105)

### Square Cities (page 104)

1. JUNCTION;
2. PRESIDIO;
3. TORNILLO;
4. SARAGOSA;
5. MARATHON;
6. SHERWOOD.

### West Texas Crossword
(page 105)

Midland, Odessa, El Paso

148

Answer Key

# Part III

## He Said What? (page 112)

"I STILL THINK PROBABLY THE ONLY THING I'M SUITED FOR IS BEING A BOY FROM TEXAS."

### Neighbors Crossword (page 110)

### State Parks Crossword (page 120)

### Texas U Alumni Word Search (page 118)

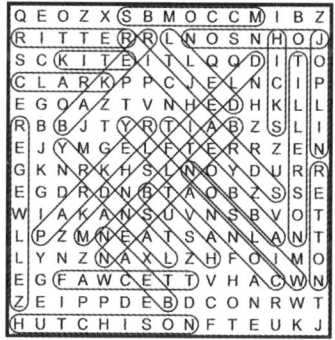

### Concert Venues Crossword (page 124)

### Lone Star Crossword (page 116)

### Colleges Crossword (page 128)

# Texas Crosswords

## Playhouse Sudoku (page 130)

## History Crossword (page 134)

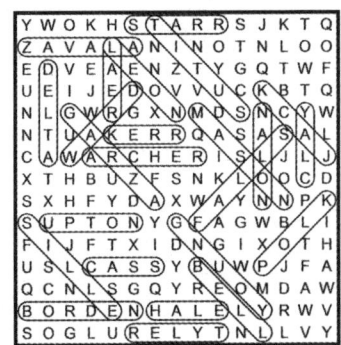

## MFAH (page 130)

MHFA, FAMH, AHFM.

## Texas Time Line (page 133)

1. 1682;
2. 1845;
3. 1963;
4. 1954;
5. 1766;
6. 2001;
7. 1832;
8. 1917;
9. 1883;
10. 1960.

## Counties Word Search (page 136)